Spiritual Friendship

The Classic Text
with a Spiritual
Commentary by
Dennis Billy, C.Ss.R.

Classics with Commentary, a series in the Christian Classics line devoted to rediscovering classic Christian literature, mines the depths of the rich tradition of Christian spirituality. Critical translations accompanied by timely and accessible commentary and probing questions revitalize these works for another generation of spiritual pilgrims.

Books in the Classics with Commentary series

- *The Imitation of Christ* by Thomas à Kempis
- *Interior Castle* by Teresa of Avila
- *Visits to the Most Holy Sacrament and to Most Holy Mary* by Alphonsus de Liguori
- *Spiritual Friendship* by Aelred of Rievaulx

CLASSICS
with
COMMENTARY

Spiritual Friendship

The Classic Text with a Spiritual Commentary by Dennis Billy, C.Ss.R.

Aelred of Rievaulx

Christian Classics ✦ *Notre Dame, Indiana*

Founded in 1865, Ave Maria Press is a ministry of the United States Province of Holy Cross.

www.christian-classics.com

ISBN-10 0-87061-242-5   ISBN-13 978-0-87061-242-8

Cover and text design by John R. Carson.

Cover photo: Erich Lessing / Art Resource, NY.

Printed and bound in the United States of America.

In memory of

my good friend in Christ

J. Alan Groves (1952–2007)

A man of the Word,

A man of God,

A man of many friends

Here we are, you and I, and I hope a third, Christ, is in our midst.

—Aelred of Rievaulx

Contents

Introduction

✛

Aelred of Rievaulx (1110–1167) was a twelfth-century Cistercian abbot and well-known spiritual writer, whose treatise, *Spiritual Friendship*,[1] is widely considered a classic of Christian spirituality. Inspired by Roman statesman and orator Marcus Tullius Cicero's philosophical dialogue, *On Friendship*,[2] Aelred approaches his subject from a decidedly religious standpoint, examining both the theoretical and practical aspects of friendship in the light of faith in Christ. Christian friendship, he maintains, is all about extending the fellowship of Christ to another. The more two persons grow as friends, the more they should sense the gentle, unobtrusive, yet abiding presence of this quiet third partner in their lives. He affirms this belief when talking to his friend Ivo at the outset of Book One, stating "Here we are, you and I, and I hope a third, Christ, in our midst."[3]

Plan and Purpose

When writing his treatise, Aelred follows the dialogue format used by Tullius (as Cicero is also called). Although popular and widely used in both classical antiquity and much of Christian history, this literary genre seldom appears in today's religious literature. When first encountered, it may seem complicated, and even a bit off-putting. Rather than developing a particular argument in a straightforward, linear fashion, a dialogue, as its name suggests, proceeds by way of discussion, with two or more characters often presenting different points of view in their search for truth. When reading a dialogue, a person does not follow a single line of reasoning, but engages in a lively conversation. At its best, dialogue invites the reader to become more than an isolated thinker—he or she becomes an active participant in a group discovery.[4]

In our present time, unfortunately, a sense of active engagement offered by dialogue has the potential to be somewhat dulled by the reader's lack of familiarity with the literary form, as well as by the distant historical and cultural context in which Aelred wrote. As such, one of my main purposes in offering a commentary embedded in the text is to offset this unfortunate handicap by helping today's reader enter into the dialogue more easily, and thus discover its freshness and present relevance. In seeking to make Aelred's teaching more accessible, I examine each of the treatise's three books in detail, draw helpful distinctions, and clarify its insights. I do so without compromising Aelred's thought and, for this reason, include Sr. Mary Eugenia Laker's classic English translation for those who wish to benefit more directly from his discourse.[5] I also pose pertinent questions to help readers probe his thought still further and discover its relevance for their own lives. By examining the work in this way, I hope to encourage others to recognize the value of Aelred's teaching on friendship and to see it as an important dimension for growth in the spiritual life today.

Aelred's Life and Writings

Most of what we know about Aelred's life comes from Walter Daniel's *The Life of Aelred of Rievaulx*, which appeared shortly after the abbot's death in 1167, and the scant autobiographical information that Aelred provides in his own works.[6] Aelred was born in 1110 in Hexham in Northumberland near the border with Scotland. He was the son of Eilaf, a married priest, who came from a long line of priestly ancestors whose hereditary charge was to serve as the guardian of the shrine of St. Cuthbert at the cathedral in Durham. However, with the arrival of the Gregorian Reform movement in the mid-eleventh century and its strict demands for priestly celibacy, the days of the married clergy in the Western Church were numbered. In 1083, Aelred's grandfather left Durham for Hexham after the local bishop put the shrine under the charge of monks from Jarrow and instructed the married clergy either to become monks or leave. In 1113, Hexham itself was given over to the care of Augustinian canons, and Aelred's father was left with scant funds to meet his family's needs. In 1138, after years of hardship and dwindling resources, Aelred's father surrendered his remaining claims to Hexham and at his death became a professed member of the monastic community of St. Cuthbert at Durham.

The change of fortunes in Aelred's family due to mandatory celibacy for clergy did not negatively affect Aelred's education or career. Aelred came from a learned family, with strong ties to the noble class. He probably began his education with a tutor at Hexham and then continued it in a school at Durham. At the age of fourteen or fifteen, he was sent to the court of King David I of Scotland to further his education as a member of the nobility. Aelred thrived in his new surroundings and, before long, found himself charged with a position of responsibility, possibly that of steward of the king's table. Aelred remained at court for roughly nine years, and it was probably during this time that he first read Cicero's *On Friendship*. This work would have a lasting impression on him and provide a model for his own treatment of the subject.

Although Aelred was successful and popular at the king's court, he appears to have been unhappy with his life of luxury, discontent with the superficial nature of his ties, and yearning for something more. In 1134, while on his return from a mission to the archbishop of York, Aelred had occasion to visit the newly established Cistercian monastery of Rievaulx. This monastery had been founded just two years earlier through the monks of Citeaux and the sponsorship of a local lord, Walter Espec. Aelred was so impressed with what he saw that within two days he found himself again at the monastery gate seeking admission.

A man of Aelred's high social caliber, and with such sincere and honest intent, was welcomed with open arms by the fledgling community at Rievaulx. Gaining entrance into a monastery, however, was one thing; perseverance in the monastic life was quite another. The transition from courtly life to the strict rigors of the Cistercian following of Benedictine monasticism was no doubt very difficult for Aelred. Many of the pleasures of life to which he had grown accustomed while at the king's court were now no longer available. In the monastery, he was given the bare essentials for a life completely dedicated to the perennial praise of God through liturgy and the recitation of the psalms, manual labor, and spiritual reading. For Aelred, the contrast between before and after could not have been greater. What he gave up by way of earthly comfort, however, was replaced by the deep inner peace that the Cistercian life evoked. Aelred rose to the occasion and made this new, demanding, yet spiritually enticing world his own. He flourished in his new monastic setting just as he did at the court of King David.

For the most part, Aelred spent his first nine years in the monastery as a novice and professed monk. In 1142, he was sent to Rome as the representative of the abbot to represent the monastery's position concerning the elected successor of the archbishop of York. On his way back to England, it is possible that he found his way to Clairvaux and made the acquaintance of St. Bernard. Upon his return to Rievaulx, he was made novice master of the monastery, a position that he kept for a relatively short period of time. In 1143, he was chosen to lead a group of monks to establish a new monastery at Revesby. Four years later, in 1147, he was elected abbot of Rievaulx, a position he would hold until his death in 1167.

As a writer, Aelred left behind a substantial body of work noted for its quality and breadth of insight. His spiritual works include: *The Mirror of Charity* (1142–43), *Jesus at the Age of Twelve* (1153–57), *A Rule of Life for a Recluse* (1160–66), *The Pastoral Prayer* (1163–66), *Dialogue on the Soul* (1163–66), *Spiritual Friendship* (1164–67), and several collections of sermons. His historical works include: *The Genealogy of the Kings of England* (1153–54), *The Battle of the Standard* (1155), and *The Life of Saint Edward the Confessor* (1163). His hagiographical works include: *The Life of Saint Ninian* (1154–60), *The Saints of Hexham* (c. 1155), and *The Nun of Watton* (1158–65). A collection of about three hundred of his letters, moreover, survived in England until the fifteenth century.[7]

Aelred's Spiritual and Theological Outlook

Aelred's spiritual and theological outlook relates closely to his Cistercian vocation. The Cistercians were a late-eleventh-century reform of Benedictine monasticism. Founded at Citeaux (Burgundy) in 1098 by Robert of Molesme with twenty companions, their basic approach to monasticism was to reject anything not stated explicitly in the Benedictine Rule. Although the community had a rough beginning and was at one point even in danger of extinction, its fortunes were greatly enhanced by Bernard of Clairvaux (1090-1153), who entered Citeaux in 1112 with a group of thirty noble companions. Bernard would become one of the most influential churchmen of his day and was a great promoter of the Cistercians. During his lifetime he oversaw a remarkable expansion of the order and eventually became known as its second founder.[8]

The Cistercians were monastic rigorists and interpreted St. Benedict's Rule to the letter. They clothed themselves solely according to what was explicitly stated: a tunic of wool, a cowl of the same material, and a scapular for work. They slept on mats with only a pillow and a blanket of wool for bedding. Their daily lives centered around common prayer, private devotion, and manual labor. Rejecting all revenues of an ecclesiastical or feudal nature, they built their monasteries in uninhabited forests or marshlands where, with the help of lay coadjutors known as *conversi*, they settled or reclaimed many of the interior regions of Europe. The Cistercians simplified the divine worship (*opus dei*), stripping from it centuries of liturgical accretions. They also did away with elaborate church art: crosses of gold or silver were not permitted; chalices could only be of silver; liturgical vestments such as chasubles and albs could not contain ornaments of silver, silk, or gold; their architecture and interior furnishings were simple but tasteful. All in all, the Cistercians wanted to reconcile the text of the Rule of Benedict with their private spiritual lives, their worship, and their source of revenue. They tried to restore the balance of work and prayer so highly regarded in the Rule. Their liturgy, work, prayer, and even their legislation were all an attempt to preserve to the best of their ability the letter of the Rule.[9]

As monks, the Cistercians were also deeply influenced by the monastic approach to theology. Monastic theology was an extension of the patristic tradition. Its goal was compunction, the desire of heaven, the wisdom gained from a true Christian gnosis. According to M.D. Chenu, it "was an anticipation of paradise where all dialectic would be ludicrous, where wisdom would absorb all science, even sacred science."[10] In the twelfth century, Bernard of Clairvaux was one the great representatives of the monastic approach to theology. Aelred, whom his own contemporaries called the "Bernard of the North," was another.[11]

Monastic theology had five major characteristics. In the first place, it was *experiential*. The monk desired a personal knowledge of God and used learning as a means of achieving it. For this reason, prayer and study were inexorably linked. Through them, the monk came to a deeper understanding of himself and was thus able to give greater praise and glory to God. By contemplating the mysteries contained in Holy Writ, creation, and the human soul, the monk sought a close affective union with his creator.

In the second place, monastic theology was *symbolic*. The Neo-Platonic background of monastic thought enabled the cloister dweller to view all of reality as a visible reflection of God's glory. Everything functioned as a symbol of another reality and expressed both a similarity and a difference with its transcendent referent. The nondemonstrative method of monastic theology was closely linked with *meditatio* and *allegoria* (literally, "to say something other"). The symbols discovered in creation, Holy Writ, and the liturgy (not to mention the human soul) carried the monk toward the contemplation of the divine mysteries.

In the third place, monastic theology was *traditionalist*. It was very cautious of any attempts to change the symbolic system arranged for the expressed purpose of leading the monk to an experience of and ultimate union with the divine. This does not mean that the monk held a static view of the past or that he could not think progressively in concrete situations. It did mean, however, that he was terribly wary of novelty for novelty's sake, especially when it came to formulations concerning the divine mysteries. Because the monk used the symbols of theology *to lead him to an experience of God*, he was very hesitant to change them simply to make them more rational and systematic.

In the fourth place, monastic theology emphasized *the epistemological role of love*. Love's power to unite heightens the monk's desire for God and brings about in him a connatural knowledge of the divine. This intuitive knowledge brings with it moments of intense insight that reveal a deep sharing in the life of the divine. These insights come to the individual by the inner illuminating light of God and contribute to his interior, spiritual growth. The affective life of the monk was thus intimately tied to his intellectual activity. Reason and will worked together in the closest harmony; love could understand what the mind often could not even begin to comprehend.

Finally, monastic theology placed *limitations on the use of reason and secular learning*. Reason, it was thought, could get in the way of theology's clearly stated purpose of union with God. Vain curiosity could distract the monk from prayer. The concern for clarity could move spiritual experience to the periphery of theological thought. Argument and speculation could replace growth in charity as the purpose of learning. For reasons such as these, secular knowledge was thought to have little value in itself and was considered useful only to the extent that it helped the monk in his spiritual journey. It was to be used with extreme caution and, at all times, submitted with care to the traditional judgments of faith.[12]

Aelred's spiritual outlook was affected by all of the above. The physical rigorism that led the Cistercians to settle Europe's interior wastelands reflected an inner conviction that the whole universe needed to be reclaimed for God, especially the wild and unruly nature of man. Putting down roots in these harsh, forboding places pointed to an interior journey where the savage and unruly passions of the soul had to be confronted and tamed. Aelred's reflection on his own personal experience was a primary source for his spiritual teaching. Along with traditional sources of scripture and the writings of the Church Fathers (especially St. Augustine), it provides a fundamental point of reference for gauging progress in the spiritual life. Aelred wanted to experience God, not merely learn about him. He believed that creation was rife with symbols that reflected the identity of a loving and compassionate creator. Love, in his mind, was both the way of God and the way to God. It offered a knowledge of God that came not through intellectual concepts, but through a connatural union of wills. Friendship, he believed, was a way in which this love could be experienced on earth. Impressed as he was by the learning in a secular work such as Cicero's *On Friendship*, he was well aware of its inherent weaknesses and set out to write his own treatise on friendship precisely because he believed that the Christian faith could transform human friendship and raise it to new heights.

Aelred's spiritual vision represented the best that the Cistercians and the monastic approach to theology could offer and flowed into his vision of the cosmos, Church, and society. For him, the universe and everything in it was created according to a hierarchical pattern by a loving and caring God. Man is a microcosm of this cosmos, and his fall from grace had repercussions throughout the whole created order. The great disfigurement of sin is rectified by the refiguration of grace made possible through Christ's redeeming action. As a result of this action, the wounds of human nature are healed and people are able to move away from their self-centeredness and walk once more in a humble, loving relationship with God and one another.[13]

The Church, for Aelred, is the fellowship of saints in heaven and on earth. It enjoys communion with God, yet is still on a pilgrim journey; it is a reflection of God's intrinsic unity and his concern for humanity's welfare. Aelred distinguishes three fundamental orders in the Church (clerics, monks, and laity), but introduces many variations within them (solitaries, monks, regular canons, secular clergy, and married and unmarried laity). All are called to embody the Christian virtues, especially love, humility, and patience. The Church possesses a hierarchy of order (bishops, priests, deacons) and a hierarchy of holiness (monks, clergy, laity). These holy ranks complement each other and are important for the life and governance of Church and society. They reflect the hierarchical pattern embedded in all of reality, including the hierarchical ordering of divine love itself.[14]

When he entered Rievaulx in 1134, Aelred made a fundamental choice about the direction his life would take. This decision marks a turning point, and reveals many of his core beliefs about the spiritual life. For one thing, he turned his back on the world and a promising ecclesiastical or courtly career to embrace a life that was both physically demanding and devoted to the perennial praise of God through the recitation of the psalms, spiritual reading, and manual labor. He did so because his desire for God was so strong that it outweighed all worldly considerations and led him to embrace a way of life that was most conducive to his own personal conversion. Entering the monastery, for Aelred, was not a condemnation of the world he left behind, but a genuine response to a heartfelt call to turn his life completely over to God and to participate in the building of God's kingdom on earth that life in the monastery represented.

The monastery, for Aelred, was a beacon of light in a world immersed in shadow and darkness. It pointed to a world yet to come, but already present. This eschatological, "already-but-not-yet" character of monastic life permeates much of his writing and has a great deal of significance for his treatise on friendship. The cloister was a greenhouse where the seeds of the kingdom could swell, sprout, and reach fruition. Within its cloister walls, it was possible for true friendship in Christ to take root, deepen, and mature. These close, intimate bonds were concrete signs of God's loving presence in the world, and mirrored those of the kingdom.

Spiritual Friendship

Although Aelred wrote *Spiritual Friendship* (1163–64) late in life, the work stands in continuity with his earlier spiritual writings. This is true especially with regard to his first work, *The Mirror of Charity* (1142–43), which he wrote at the request of Bernard of Clairvaux to provide a firm theological foundation for the Cistercian life. This treatise contains in germ form the key insights into the nature of love that would come to full term in later works such as *Spiritual Friendship*. Its theme is that the Cistercian life embraces Christ's cross, a yoke made easy to bear through love, which in turn is generated by the cross. In many ways, Aelred's treatise on friendship is nothing but a deeper development of this single intuition.[15]

Aelred's theory of love as expressed in *The Mirror of Charity* provides an important backdrop for understanding his theory of spiritual friendship. His approach focuses on the threefold experience of what he terms *attraction*, *intention*, and *fruition*.[16] *Attraction* has to do with the immediate, desirable effect that someone or something has on the mind. This effect occurs naturally and comes from the sensible impressions made on the mind by the outside world. *Intention*, by way of contrast, concerns the will's inclination toward a particular person or object. It comes about by a decision to pursue someone or something as a specific goal. *Fruition* results from this decision and concerns our enjoyment of the benefits of the desired person or object. This enjoyment is the fruit of attaining that for which we long.[17] To cite one simple example: I see a cup of water and am drawn to it (*Attraction*); I move toward it and pick it up, because I have decided to drink it (*Intention*); I quench my thirst and experience delight (*Fruition*).

In a world without sin, these three elements of love would be unhindered in their movement toward the good. In a world corrupted, however, by humanity's fall from grace, the powers of the soul have been weakened, and it is possible for any of these elements to tend toward evil.[18] To put it another way: I can feel an attraction toward the idea of robbing a stranger (*Evil Attraction*); I can freely choose to rob a particular stranger (*Evil Inclination*); and I can enjoy the money gained from the successful robbery (*Evil Fruition*). For Aelred, only the power of Christ's redeeming grace can heal the weakened powers of the soul and enable a person to love in a way commensurate to the dignity of his nature. This grace transforms our intellectual pride into humility and heals our defective wills so that we can love.

With regard to friendship, grace enables us to see ourselves as we truly are, and befriend someone in a way that our attraction to, inclination towards, and enjoyment of him or her are upright and well ordered. *Spiritual Friendship* demonstrates how the love of friends, healed by grace, mirrors the love of God. The work contains both theoretical material about the nature of Christian friendship, as well as practical suggestions about how to deal with difficulties that invariably arise among friends.

Spiritual Friendship is composed of a Prologue and three Books. The Prologue introduces the work through a brief autobiographical note and a statement of Aelred's purpose for writing the treatise. Book One deals with the origin and nature of friendship. In it, Aelred talks with Ivo, a younger monk of the monastery, about the origins of true friendship. He uses Cicero's definition of friendship as a point of departure, yet finds Cicero's definition lacking the insights of divine revelation (namely, the revelation that true friendship, like all things worthwhile, begins and ends in Christ). Aelred goes on to discuss the various types of friendship and arrives at a threefold distinction: the carnal, the worldly, and the spiritual. He also examines the relationship between charity and friendship, and concludes that they were united before Adam's fall, separated after it, and are destined to be rejoined in the kingdom to come. During our time on earth, charity can exclude friendship, but friendship can never exclude charity.[19]

Book Two focuses on the fruit and perfection of friendship. It takes place some years later. Ivo is dead, and Aelred now enters into conversation with two younger monks of his monastery named Walter and Gratian. Walter has read the recently discovered paper containing Aelred's original discussion with Ivo, and now wishes to know more about the fruition of friendship. Gratian's appearance widens the discussion and brings some welcome light comic relief to the conversation.

In the course of their discussion, Aelred tells Walter and Gratian that true friendship is eternal and bears fruit in both this life and the next. He likens the various stages of friendship to a threefold kiss: the carnal, the spiritual, and the intellectual (what today we would call the "mystical"). The first is physical; the second, a mingling of the spirits of two friends; the third, a mingling of a person's spirit with the Spirit of God. He goes on to say that only the good can become true spiritual friends, and that Christ demonstrated the proper limits of friendship when he laid down his life. Aelred cites many examples from scripture to support his claims.[20]

Book Three continues the discussion of Aelred, Walter, and Gratian, and deals with the conditions necessary for unbroken friendship. It is by far the longest and most practical of the three books. In it, Aelred talks with Walter and Gratian about the various stages by which two people become friends. These include: selection, probation, admission, and perfect harmony of life. With regard to the selection of potential friends, Aelred outlines the various vices that would disqualify a person as a candidate for spiritual friendship, and goes into detail about dissolving a "friendship" in the initial stages once its lack of authenticity becomes clear. When speaking about probation (the "testing" of a potential friend), he describes the various qualities to be tested in a candidate for friendship. While the idea of testing potential friends might seem strange to modern readers, for Aelred it is essential. Spiritual friendship, he maintains, is so important for our lives that we should not enter into it lightly, and likewise should be very careful when selecting our friends and testing their worthiness. When discussing admission, Aelred outlines the qualities that need to be continually fostered, and describes how one should go about cultivating them so that friends will live in communion with each other and achieve true harmony of life. All during this time, Walter and Gratian raise objections and ask for clarifications. Aelred, in turn, cites examples from sacred scripture, the Church Fathers, and his own personal experience to clarify matters.[21]

Dennis J. Billy, C.Ss.R.

How to Read Spiritual Friendship

✢

Although this brief summary does little justice to Aelred's profound insights and depth, it highlights the comprehensive nature of the treatise and its value as a guidebook for Christian friendship. In order to help the reader better appreciate the treatise, what follows is a series of "interpretative filters" or "lenses" that can help us to understand Aelred's teaching and find its relevance for our own lives. These "lenses" bring to the fore some of our most basic ideas about the nature of Christian friendship, and will help us to see the similarities (and the dissimilarities) between our world and Aelred's. They remind us, moreover, that our goal in reading a book such as this should not be to lose ourselves in a nostalgic recreation of a distant (and ultimately irretrievable) medieval religious landscape, but to explore that past in order to find helpful insights for dealing with our present spiritual struggles. They encourage us to enter into a dialogue with the text, and to become aware of our own feelings and judgments about the meaning of our spiritual journey. In doing so, we will doubtless find ourselves, at times, both questioning the teaching of *Spiritual Friendship* and being questioned by it. This dynamic relationship between the text and its reader touches the very heart of spiritual reading, and is extremely important when dealing with a classic of spirituality such as this. For our present purposes, seven of these "interpretative filters" or "lenses" are especially worth mentioning.

Filter One. To begin with, when reading the treatise, we should keep in mind Aelred's monastic background and not expect everything he says to be immediately applicable to those who live outside cloister walls. Although Aelred's teaching on friendship has universal appeal, we need to remember that he believed the world was a very dangerous place, and that he thought the monastery provided the best environment for spiritual friendship to take root and develop. As a Cistercian dedicated to living the Benedictine Rule to the letter, he would have been very conscious that the monastery was meant to be a "school for God's service," and that those in it sought to lead lives of conversion.[22] Everything Aelred says about friendship must be understood in this light.

Forming sound Christian friendships, Aelred believed, was one of the things monks could learn within the cloister to help them along the way of conversion. The dedication to work, prayer, and spiritual reading, the focus on communal life, and the regular monastic order gave them the opportunity to foster a contemplative attitude toward life that would both change them and spill over into their relationships with others. Even within the monastery, however, Aelred was keenly aware that forming authentic Christian friendships was difficult work and required discretion, dedication, and discerning action. When reading his treatise, we need to find ways of adapting his insights to fit our present circumstances. Although relatively few receive the call to monastic life, all of us are called to find practical structures that will help us to serve, lead lives of conversion, and enter into authentic relationships with others. When reading *Spiritual Friendship,* rather than asking what it would be like for us to cultivate friendship in some imagined monastery, we need instead to ask how our present friendships are (or are not) helping to cultivate deeper conversion.

Filter Two. As pointed out earlier, Cicero's work *On Friendship* influenced Aelred deeply and provided much of the form and content for the treatise. Cicero's insights into the nature of friendship got Aelred interested in the topic as a youth and were remembered years later when he felt inspired to write about friendship for his fellow monks. Aware of the limitations of the classical Greek and Roman authors, however, Aelred demonstrates both a capacity and a willingness to go beyond Cicero's insights on friendship, and to root his own teaching in specifically Christian sources. To this end, he fills his writing with many references from both the Old and New Testaments so as to anchor his teaching solidly in the spirit of Christ. From the Old Testament, he cites numerous examples of friendship from the historical books, and many wise sayings on friendship from the Wisdom books. From the New Testament, he likes to refer to the Gospel of John, as well as to St. Paul's teaching on God's unconditional love for humanity.

In addition to the scriptures, Aelred makes good use of the Church fathers, especially Augustine's *Confessions,* a particular favorite. Moreover, he supplements these references to classical and Christian sources with many of his own personal experiences of friendship. Aelred's willingness to offer examples from his own life brings an added personal dimension to the treatise, and gives it a quality of practical, lived experience. Aelred is not a slave to his sources, but uses them to forge his own unique work that is continuous with the best of what classical literature, Christian revelation, and his own personal experience have to offer. He uses his sources in a way that allows him to put his own imprint on the treatise's form and content. In this respect, Aelred does not merely summarize what went before him, but provides his own unique synthesis that adds to the tradition and moves it forward. When reading Aelred's treatise, we should be aware of the sources that have influenced us in our own understanding of friendship. What books, what passages from scripture, what people, what personal experiences have shaped the way we approach our relationships with others? How do we prioritize them? How do we use them? Do we simply repeat what they are saying? Have we mastered them enough to incorporate them into our own unique synthesis?[23]

Filter Three. When reading Aelred's treatise on friendship, we should remember that he specifically chose to write it as a dialogue, and that the content of his message is intimately related to the form in which he expresses it. Although dialogue was a popular literary form for writers of Aelred's day,[24] his main reason for selecting it was probably the formative influence on him of Cicero's earlier work. *On Friendship* was written as a dialogue; as such, it makes sense that Aelred would write his own work in the same literary genre. Doing so would have been a sign of respect for the insights of the Roman philosopher who inspired him, as well as a way of situating himself within a particular literary and philosophical tradition.

When reading a dialogue, it is important to keep track of the various lines of conversation, so as not to lose sight of the main movement of the discourse. As with Cicero's dialogue, Aelred's dynamic is relatively simple: in Book One, he has but a single dialogue partner, Ivo; in Book Two, he has two, Walter and Gratian. Their conversation is dignified and respectful, sometimes humorous and playful, and best characterized by an intense desire for truth and holiness. This simplicity carries with it an important message: friendship begins with a simple dialogue between two people who respect one another and have learned to listen to each other. It extends beyond their lifetimes (in Book Two, Aelred fondly remembers his old friend, the now long-deceased Ivo) and is open to forming new relationships (hence, the appearance of Walter and Gratian). What is more, even though Aelred is abbot of the monastery and the religious superior of those with whom he is talking, he does not talk down to his friends. He relates to them as equals in the best sense of the word. When reading a dialogue such as Aelred's, we should try to imagine the conversation in our minds in a way that reflects the contemplative and respectful spirit of those involved. Among other things, we should ask ourselves if we know how to be present to our friends, if we truly listen to them, and if we relate to them as equals.[25]

Filter Four. We also need to be conscious of the meditative approach to reading that was common in medieval monasteries and was simply accepted by Aelred. Along with prayer and manual labor, spiritual reading (*lectio divina*) was an integral part of the daily monastic routine. Monks would spend many hours each day reflecting upon passages from scripture, the Church Fathers, and other works of Christian literature. For them, depth of insight was more important than the amount read. They believed that beneath the literal meaning of a text, spiritual senses existed that would manifest themselves to the monk when he chewed the words around in his mind and thoroughly digested them. The goal of this spiritual mastication of the text was to break through a passage's external crust and to feed on the spiritual food within. This interpretative approach was generally allegorical in nature. An external hierarchy of being formed the basis of an internal hierarchy of meaning beneath the words of a text. This hidden, spiritual truth could be found in scripture, in the Book of Nature, in the apocalyptic movement of history, in Christian and pagan literature, and in the veritable summit of earthly existence—the Liturgy. In each of these spheres, the monastic reader embarked on a spiritual pilgrimage. His journey through the many possible levels of meaning in a text was itself a spiritual representation of his mounting the external hierarchy of being through which, by the grace of God, he merited salvation and reached his eternal reward.

Out of respect for the philosophical nature of *On Friendship*, Aelred rarely provides *Spiritual Friendship* with the kind of extended allegorical interpretations found in many of his other spiritual writings. At the same time, he had certain expectations of how his treatise on friendship would be read and interpreted. He knew it would be carefully studied, savored, and chewed for the hidden truth that would rise up within the reader's heart in a moment of contemplative insight. He knew that the words of the text would be perceived as an external crust to be penetrated for its hidden meaning. In light of such expectations, the treatise should be read not only for its content (however important), but also for the spiritual truth that it contains within. We would do well to take a similar interpretative approach to the treatise as a text meant not merely to elucidate a particular teaching about Christian friendship, but to be a means of spiritual growth. In doing so, we should look to the text for relevant insights about the theory and practice of friendship that both inspire us and are directly applicable to our own lives.[26]

Filter Five. Aelred's hierarchical vision of the universe is very different from our present worldview, and needs to be appropriately unpacked. In the medieval world, "hierarchy" was a fundamentally positive word used by Christians to conceptualize the way in which God organized the cosmos and everything in it. The philosophical justification for the hierarchical understanding of the universe came from Neo-Platonism, a systematization of Platonic thought, itself hierarchical, that was "baptized" and adapted for Christian purposes, most famously seen in the theology of St. Augustine. Since the thought of Augustine had such a strong impact on the Latin West, especially in monastic circles, it should not be surprising to see this hierarchical vision of reality reflected in Aelred's understanding of the universe, human society, the Church, human nature, and holiness. For Aelred, monastic life rested at the top of the hierarchy of holiness. In a fallen world darkened by sin, it was, of all ways of life, the most conducive to the single-hearted pursuit of virtue and holiness.

In today's postmodern world, "hierarchy" is rarely (if ever) used as a comprehensive organizing concept for reality. Over time, it has become a much more ambivalent concept, one that still maintains a powerful presence in the way the Church and many societies and institutions are organized, but one that also can stir deep contrary emotions of anger, suspicion, and resentment. When reading Aelred, we need to be aware of the hierarchical underpinnings of the treatise and take them into account when forming our own judgments about his teaching on friendship. We should do so especially in light of the Second Vatican Council's teaching on the universal call to holiness and its recognition of each vocational state as a unique way to God.

At the same time, we would do well to allow ourselves to be challenged by the comprehensive claims of Aelred's distant worldview, and seriously ask ourselves what, if anything, we have found to take their place. To put it another way, we would do well to ask ourselves if there is anything we can learn from this worldview that could help us construct viable spiritual cures to offset the growing cancers of human degradation, intellectual relativism, unbridled consumerism, and the abuse of the environment— evils that are spreading at an alarming rate in our increasingly globalized world.[27]

Filter Six. It has been said that all mature theological reflection involves an interaction of our understanding of God, human existence, and the world. Aelred's treatise on spiritual friendship is no exception. His God is the compassionate and loving creator of the universe. Although its powers of body and soul have been corrupted by the Fall, humanity as God envisioned it remains fundamentally intact, and has been redeemed by the elevating power of Christ's Passion, Death, and Resurrection. Even though the world has been corrupted by Adam's sin and has become a dark and dangerous abode, it, too, has been touched by the redemptive and regenerating action of Christ. The story of humanity and the world is thus one of creation, fall, and redemption.

For Aelred, the present historical epoch is a time of waiting for Christ's second coming when the full effects of the new creation begun in Christ's paschal mystery will become manifest. In his mind, spiritual friendship is a visible sign of this kingdom to come. It makes present in a blessed few what one day will be shared by everyone. It points to the time when charity and friendship—closely related at creation, but divided after the Fall—will come together again and resound with joy in the presence of God. When reading Aelred's treatise on spiritual friendship, we need to ask ourselves about our own understanding of God, humanity, and the world. We need to ask ourselves what we think about these realities and how they interact. We also need to ask ourselves how our understanding of God, humanity, and the world relates to the Christian teaching on humanity's fall and redemption by Christ. Aelred's treatise is intimately tied to a larger framework of ideas inspired by the Christian message. To benefit fully from his teaching today, we need to develop a way of determining what is essential to that framework, and what can be changed or adapted to our present historical circumstances.[28]

Filter Seven. Finally, some of Aelred's insights into the Christian understanding of human existence were very innovative for his day, and should be welcomed with open arms. At the same time, we should be careful not to project onto his writings concepts and distinctions that were not of his own making, and would have been foreign to his worldview. On the one hand, his position on the relationship between men and women was very creative for his day, especially since he lived in a hierarchically organized world that typically placed men over women in positions of authority. In Book One, when commenting on the creation of man and woman, Aelred embraces a view that stands in stark contrast with many of his contemporaries. He says that woman was taken from man's side to show that human beings "are equal and, as it were, collateral and that there is in human affairs neither a superior nor an inferior, a characteristic of true friendship."[29] Such a statement was very original for the twelfth century, and should be hailed as an example of an alternative medieval vision of the relationship between man and woman.

On the other hand, some recent scholarship on Aelred has used references in his works to claim that he was homosexual in his sexual orientation. The response to these studies has been both mixed and steeped in controversy. After reading the various positions, one can only conclude at present that the question of Aelred's homosexuality cannot be proven one way or the other. At the same time, some scholars have wondered if the correct questions are being posed by concentrating on such matters. The real focus of interest, they say, should be not on Aelred's sexual orientation, but on what he teaches about spiritual friendship. When reading his treatise on friendship, we should try our best to focus on this one central concern and not get caught up in issues that can easily sidetrack us and move us off the point. In such a context, we will then ask ourselves about the nature of friendships among all: men, women, heterosexuals, and homosexuals. Reflecting seriously on such topics would be much more in the spirit of Aelred than would poring over his biography and insights simply to identify his sexual orientation.[30]

Conclusion

Aelred of Rievaulx's *Spiritual Friendship* numbers among the great works of Christian literature on friendship. Completed in the years just prior to his death, it offers a thorough understanding of the nature of Christian friendship, and some very practical advice about how such relationships should be begun and cultivated. Using Cicero's famous dialogue, *On Friendship*, as an inspiration, and incorporating insights from scripture, the fathers of the Church, and his own experience, Aelred provides his readers with many profound insights into the importance of friendship for a person's well-being.

Aelred's teaching on friendship, and his lively conversations with Ivo, Walter, and Gratian, encourage us to examine the quality of our own personal relationships. By adapting the dialogue form to suit his practical, experiential concerns for entering into the friendship of Christ, Aelred presents us with a number of possibilities regarding the range of spiritual friendships available. He urges us, at least implicitly, to be aware of our own potential for entering into and maintaining such relationships. By engaging the imagination, and helping the other characters of the dialogue to do the same, he raises questions, makes suggestions, and opens possibilities that inspire us to embark on a similar process of reflection.

Aelred's main interest in writing this treatise is to help us to foster intimate friendships among ourselves and with Christ. We do not journey long into the dialogue, however, before discovering that the two kinds of relationships are intimately related—and in a circular way. Spiritual friendships lead those involved to an intimate relationship with Christ. Christ, in turn, makes such relationships possible, and orients them from the very beginning toward himself. Spiritual friendships, in other words, ". . . begin in Christ, continue in Christ, and are perfected in Christ."[31] They lie at the heart of Aelred's spiritual doctrine, and have much to offer those who enter into constructive dialogue with their underlying literary and theological premises. Only by examining these contexts will we discover their influence on Aelred's teaching and be ready to make appropriate adaptations for today.

Dennis J. Billy, C.Ss.R.

✢

Spiritual Friendship

Aelred of Rievaulx

Translated by Mary Eugenia Laker, S.S.N.D.

✢

Spiritual Friendship

✛

An Overview

Aelred of Rievaulx's *Spiritual Friendship* is a classic work on Christian friendship. Although written more than eight centuries ago, in a cultural milieu very different from our own, it still offers many profound insights into the role of friendship for the Christian believer. For Aelred, to grow in friendship is to enter more deeply in the love and friendship of Christ. Such relationships are a primary means through which God's love comes into the world. They have a sacred, almost sacramental, quality to them that draws people closer to each other and to God. Spiritual friendships are eternal. They last forever, because they are forged in the love of one who has laid down his life for his friends (Jn 15:13).

Aelred's dialogue covers a wide range of topics concerning Christian friendship. In three relatively compact books, he deals with such issues as friendship's origins, its various kinds, its relationship to charity, the qualities one should look for in a friend, how to select and test a possible friend, how to grow in friendship, and how to deal with friendships that have gone awry. As the treatise unfolds, one gets the distinct impression that Aelred is sharing with his younger monastic confreres the fruit of a lifetime of reflection on the topic. He speaks as an authority on friendship, not simply because he has read about it and studied it in depth, but because he has forged many such relationships in his own life. He writes the treatise as a way of crystallizing his thoughts and offering his readers helpful advice on developing such lasting bonds themselves.

It bears noting that Book One differs from Books Two and Three in one very significant way. While Book One deals with largely theoretical issues about the nature and origin of friendship, Books Two and Three focus on the more practical concerns about friendship in everyday life. One of the ways that Aelred demarcates this important change of emphasis is to shift his dialogue partners from Ivo in Book One to Walter and Gratian in Books Two and Three. Another is to distance the books in time. Book One takes place long before (possibly years before) Book Two, while Books Two and Three both occur within the space of two days. The continuity throughout the treatise comes from the conversational tone of the dialogue form itself, and from Aelred's capacity to draw out the practical implications of his general theory of friendship. The result is a rich and enlightening treatment of how faith in Christ can transform one of the most basic of human relationships, and make God's love visible in our lives in very concrete, practical ways.

NB: I have provided both the Prologue and each of the three books with their own "Introduction" and series of reflection questions meant to help the reader review each book. As a further aid to the reader, and in order to make the material easier to digest, I have also taken the liberty of subdividing each of Aelred's three books into smaller units of thought, based on the numbering of the text found in the critical Latin edition. For each of these subdivisions, I have supplied relevant commentary and further questions for reflection. My goal in all of this is to make the treatise more accessible to the reader, and to assist him or her in reflecting on Aelred's words in a slow, meditative fashion.

Prologue

✛

Introduction

Aelred opens *Spiritual Friendship* with a brief Prologue that gives information about his life, and an explanation of his reasons for taking up the topic of friendship. He speaks about his early life at school, and of how he gave himself over completely to pursuing the affectionate desires of youth (see no. 1 in Aelred's text, below). He also relates how he was so driven by opposing loves and desires during that time that he often mistook them for true friendship. He says that it was not until he read Marcus Tullius Cicero's *On Friendship* that he had found something that shed light on the nature of his own relationships. Cicero's depth and eloquence helped him to understand both the real worth of friendship, and how unworthy he was at that point to become someone's friend (no. 2).

After coming into contact with the then-young Cistercian community, Aelred embraced the monastic life and, through the reading of scripture and other holy books, began to see the shallowness of all the worldly knowledge that he had accumulated in his life. Although they kept coming back to mind, even Cicero's ideas had lost much of their attraction. As a monk, Aelred saw that only Jesus and the insights of scripture could bring true meaning and happiness in life. Such thoughts made him wonder if God's revealed Word could shed any further light on the meaning of friendship. He was already aware of what many of the saints had written on friendship, and he began to think that he himself might have something to say about the topic. With this in mind, he set out to write his own work (no. 6).

Aelred ends his Prologue by explaining the structure of his treatise, imploring readers to give thanks to God for whatever benefits they may receive through it, and asking them to forgive him whatever limitations they may find (nos. 7–8). We should note that the style of his Prologue is autobiographical in nature and has much more in common with the monologue form of Augustine's Confessions than the dialogue approach adopted in the body of his treatise. It also reveals the major sources he uses in the body of his work: Cicero's treatise *On Friendship,* sacred scripture, the writings of the saints (especially St. Augustine), and his own personal experience. As far as his purpose is concerned, Aelred writes the treatise out of a genuine desire to see what friendship means in the light of Christian revelation, as well as his own need to draw up for himself "rules for a chaste and holy life" (no. 6).

✣

Text

1. When I was still just a lad at school, and the charm of my companions pleased me very much, I gave my whole soul to affection and devoted myself to love amid the ways and vices with which that age is wont to be threatened, so that nothing seemed to me more sweet, nothing more agreeable, nothing more practical, than to love.[1] 2. And so, torn between conflicting loves and friendships, I was drawn now here, now there, and not knowing the law of true friendship, I was often deceived by its mere semblance. At length there came to my hands the treatise which Tullius wrote on friendship,[2] and it immediately appealed to me as being serviceable because of the depth of his ideas, and fascination because of the charm of his eloquence. 3. And though I saw myself unfitted for that type of friendship, still I was gratified that I had discovered a formula for friendship whereby I might check the vacillations of my loves and affections.

When, in truth, it pleased our good Lord to reprove the wanderer, to lift the fallen, and with his healing touch to cleanse the leper, abandoning all worldly hopes, I entered a monastery. 4. Immediately I gave my attention to the reading of holy books, whereas prior to that, my eye, dimmed by the carnal darkness to which it had been accustomed, had not even a surface acquaintance with them. From that time on, sacred scripture became more attractive and the little learning which I had acquired in the world grew insipid in comparison. The ideas I had gathered from Cicero's treatise on friendship kept recurring to my mind, and I was astonished that they no longer had for me their wonted savor.[3] 5. For now nothing which had not been sweetened by the honey of the most sweet name of Jesus, nothing which had not been seasoned with the salt of sacred scripture, drew my affection so entirely to itself.[4] Pondering over these thoughts again and again, I began to ask myself whether they could perhaps have some support from scripture.

6. Since however I had already read many things on friendship in the writings of the saints, desiring this spiritual friendship but not being able to attain it, I decided to write my own book on spiritual friendship and to draw up for myself rules for a chaste and holy love.

7. Now, then, we have divided the work into three books: in the first, we study the nature of friendship, its source or cause; in the second we propose its fruition and excellence; in the third, we explain, to the best of our ability, how and among whom it can be preserved unbroken even to the end.[5]

8. Now, should anyone draw profit from reading this treatise, let him give thanks to God and ask for Christ's mercy upon my sins. But if anyone deems what I have written superfluous or impractical, let him pardon my unhappy position whose occupations forced me to put limits on the thought I could give to this meditation.

Dwelling in Friendship

- What do you make of Aelred's attempt to explore the contours of human friendship in the light of Christian revelation? What do you think he will find? Can you identify any of his underlying assumptions? Do you sense he is trying to conduct this investigation alone, or in the company of others? What kind of relationship does he try to establish with his readers?

- Why does Aelred put so much autobiographical material in his Prologue? What purpose does this material serve in introducing the reader to the nature of the treatise? Could he have achieved the same purpose in some other way? Does the Prologue raise any expectations about finding similar information in the main body of the treatise?

- Why does Aelred write his Prologue as a monologue, yet change to dialogue in the body of his treatise? How might dialogue be a fitting form for a treatise on friendship? How important is dialogue for our relationship with God? Does Aelred's shift from monologue to dialogue say something about its importance for our relationships with God and others? Does it say something about its importance for our relationship with ourselves?

- Of the four major sources used by Aelred—a famous pagan work (in this case, Cicero), scripture, the writings of the saints, and personal experience—which do you think he will rely upon the most? Which will he rely upon the least? What are your reasons for saying so? Which of these have had the most direct impact on your own intellectual and spiritual life?

- Does Aelred's proposed structure make sense to you? Based on your own experience, how would you develop a treatise on friendship? Would you take a different approach from Aelred? What structure would you adopt? What elements of friendship would you emphasize?

Book One

The Origin of Friendship

⊹

Book One: An Overview

In this first book, Aelred weaves a number of important themes into his text. For one thing, his selection of the dialogue form reveals something about his understanding of the nature of friendship and the search for truth. Aelred wishes not to instruct "from above," but to discuss the nature and origin of friendship with a close friend. Because Jesus is present in their midst and in the bond they share, this dialogue moves both horizontally and vertically, toward neighbor and toward God. By including Christ in the discussion, Aelred has turned the dialogue into a meditation, one we can correctly call "a prayerful conversation with God." His dialogue, in other words, involves not only his conversation with friends, but also with God. To benefit fully from it, we should read it in a slow, meditative fashion, in much the same way a monk would approach a sacred text during *lectio divina*. In such a reading, silence becomes an important mediator between the text and its reader. Through it, Jesus, the quiet and unobtrusive third partner in the dialogue, speaks to the heart and reveals deep insights into the meaning of Christian friendship.

We should also note that Aelred's ideas appear not only in those passages that he specifically attributes to himself, but at times even on the lips of his friend Ivo. For this reason, we can also say that his treatise sometimes reflects the movement of his own inner thoughts. To verify this claim, we need only to compare Aelred's words in his Prologue about how "the sweet name of Jesus" (no. 5) and the "salt of Scripture" (no. 5) are later expressed by Ivo in Book One (no 7). By placing his own thoughts in the mind and on the lips of his close friend, he conveys the close harmony of heart and mind that is so essential to those bound together in the friendship with Christ.

As in the Prologue, Aelred continues to make good use of the four main sources of his treatise. He chooses a literary form that follows closely that of Cicero's *On Friendship*. He then uses scripture, the writings of the saints, and his own personal experience of friendship in Christ to shed light on Cicero's sound-but-limited insights into human friendship. Aelred obviously gives priority to the content of his Christian sources over that of the pagan. In the Christian sources, moreover, the order of priority moves from scripture, to the writings of the saints, and lastly, to his own personal experience. Aelred, in other words, believes he speaks with more authority when quoting from scripture than when citing a saint or referring to his own experience of friendship. We would do well to keep this order of priority in mind as we go through the treatise.

In Book One, Aelred also has much to say about the relationship between charity and friendship. To understand the distinction, it is important to see that he presents it against the general background of salvation history and the doctrine of Original Sin. Before humanity's fall from grace, charity and friendship were one and universal in scope. After the fall, however, they split apart, with charity retaining its universal extension, and friendship limited to a select few. In the kingdom to come, Aelred believes that charity and friendship will again be united in Christ's love. Against this important backdrop, he speaks of a further breakup of friendship after the Fall into carnal, worldly, and spiritual relationships. In his mind, the first two focus respectively on pleasure and advantage, and are apparent, rather than true, friendships. Spiritual friendship alone is authentic and is a present-day manifestation of the kingdom to come.

For Aelred, the separation of charity and friendship after the Fall, and the further proliferation of friendship into varying types, depicts the world into which each of us is born. He believes that the need for companionship inscribed in our hearts increases with our deepening experience of life, and results in a vast spectrum of relationships that must be regulated by the carefully reasoned sanctions of law. Such governance allows true friendship to flourish by helping us grow in wisdom, transforming our inordinate passions into virtuous intentions and desires, and preventing us from being negatively influenced by any of the lesser kinds of friendship. It is reflected in the very rules of the monastery where the dialogue takes place, which indicate to Aelred and Ivo at the end of Book One that it is time to stop for the evening meal and resume the conversation at a later time.

Book One: 1–4

Introduction

Book One involves a conversation on the roots of friendship between abbot Aelred and Ivo, a younger monk of the monastery. Aelred has just finished "talking noisily" (no. 2) with a group of monks and now has some private time to devote to his friend. In his opening words to Ivo, Aelred acknowledges Jesus' presence in their midst and invites his younger confrere to open his heart and reveal what is on his mind (nos. 1–2). Ivo appreciates Aelred's sensitivity and admits that he did not say anything in the presence of the other monks because he wanted some time alone with him (no. 3).

Text

1. *Aelred.* Here we are, you and I, and I hope a third, Christ, is in our midst.[1] There is no one now to disturb us; there is no one to break in upon our friendly chat, no man's prattle or noise of any kind will creep into this pleasant solitude. Come now, beloved, open your heart, and pour into these friendly ears whatsoever you will, and let us accept gracefully the boon of this place, time, and leisure.

2. Just a little while ago as I was sitting with the brethren, while all around were talking noisily, one questioning, another arguing—one advancing some point on Sacred Scripture, another information on vices, and yet another on virtue—you alone were silent. At times you would raise your head and make ready to say something, but just as quickly, as though your voice had been trapped in your throat, you would drop your head again and continue your silence. Then you would leave us for a while, and later return looking rather

disheartened. I concluded from all this that you wanted to talk to me, but that you dreaded the crowd, and hoped to be alone with me.

3. *Ivo.*[2] That's it exactly, and I deeply appreciate your solicitude for your son. His state of mind and his desire have been disclosed to you by none other than the Spirit of Love. And would that your Lordship would grant me this favor, that, as often as you visit your sons here, I may be permitted, at least once, to have you all to myself and to disclose to you the deep feelings of my heart without disturbance.

4. *Aelred.* Indeed, I shall do that, and gladly. For I am greatly pleased to see that you are not bent on empty and idle pursuits, but that you are always speaking of things useful and necessary for your progress. Speak freely, therefore, and entrust to your friend all your cares and thoughts, that you may both learn and teach, give and receive, pour out and drink in.

Dwelling in Friendship

- How would you describe the opening setting of Book One? Although it takes place in a monastery, do you see any similarities between it and your own experience? Like Ivo, have you ever distanced yourself from a group, because you felt the need for a deeper, more personal conversation with another? Like Aelred, have you ever felt that someone else wished to have such a conversation with you? Have you ever taken the initiative to start such a conversation? If you could, how would you start such a conversation? What would you talk about?

⁘

Introduction

vo says he would like Aelred to teach him something about the origin and the end of spiritual friendship, as well as how to foster and preserve it (no. 5). Aelred replies that the Roman statesman and orator Marcus Tullius Cicero has already treated this topic in his treatise, *On Friendship,* but agrees with his friend Ivo that Cicero was unfamiliar with the nature of true friendship because he had no knowledge of Christ. He agrees to discuss the topic with Ivo, and show that true friendship begins, continues, and is perfected in Christ alone (nos. 6–9).

They start with a discussion of Cicero's definition of friendship as "a mutual harmony in affairs human and divine coupled with benevolence and charity" (no. 11). They agree that this definition, while imperfect, conveys at least some idea of the nature of friendship, and thus serves as a good point of departure (no. 17). Aelred then reflects on the similarities between the Latin words *amicus* (friend), *amor* (love), and *amicitia* (friendship), and describes friendship as a virtue that makes spirits one through bonds of love and sweetness (nos. 19, 21). He also cites St. Jerome, who claimed that true friends love one another always and that the bond between them cannot be broken (no. 24).

⁘

Text

5. *Ivo.* I am certainly ready to learn, not to teach; not to give, but to receive; to drink in, not to pour out; as indeed my youth demands of me, inexperience compels, and my religious profession exhorts. But that I may not foolishly squander on these considerations the time that I need for other matters, I wish that you would teach me something about spiritual friendship, namely, its nature and value,

its source and end, whether it can be cultivated among all, and, if not among all, then by whom; how it can be preserved unbroken, and without any disturbance of misunderstanding be brought to a holy end.

6. *Aelred.* I wonder why you think it proper to seek this information from me, since it is evident that there has been enough, and more, discussion on matters of this kind by ancient and excellent teachers; particularly since you spent your youth in studies of this sort, and have read Cicero's treatise, *On Friendship*, in which in a delightful style he treats at length all those matters which appear to pertain to friendship, and there he sets forth certain laws and precepts, so to speak, for friendship.

7. *Ivo.* That treatise is not altogether unknown to me. In fact, at one time I took great delight in it. But since I began to taste some of the sweetness from the honey comb of Holy Scripture, and since the sweet name of Christ claimed my affection for itself, whatever I henceforth read or hear, though it be treated ever so subtly and eloquently, will have no relish or enlightenment for me, if it lacks the salt of the heavenly books and the flavoring of that most sweet name.[3] 8. Therefore, those things which have already been said, even though they are in harmony with reason, and other things which the utility of this discussion demands that we treat, I should like proved to me with the authority of the Scriptures. I should like also to be instructed more fully as to how the friendship which ought to exist among us begins in Christ, is preserved according to the Spirit of Christ, and how its end and fruition are referred to Christ. For it is evident that Tullius was unacquainted with the virtue of true friendship, since he was completely unaware of its beginning and end, Christ.

9. *Aelred.* I confess I have been won over, but, not knowing myself or the extent of my own ability, I am not going to teach you anything about these matters but rather to discuss them with you. For you yourself have opened the way for both of us, and have enkindled that brilliant light on the very threshold of our inquiry, which will not allow us to wander along unknown paths, but will lead us along the sure path to the certain goal of our proposed quest.

10. For what more sublime can be said of friendship, what more true, what more profitable, than that it ought to, and is proved to, begin in Christ, continue in Christ, and be perfected in Christ? Come

now, tell me, what do you think ought to be our first consideration in this matter of friendship?

Ivo. In the first place, I think we should discuss the nature of friendship so as not to appear to be painting in emptiness, as we would, indeed, if we were unaware of the precise identity of that about which an ordered discussion on our part should proceed.

11. *Aelred.* But surely you are satisfied, as a starting point, with what Tullius says, are you not? "Friendship is mutual harmony in affairs human and divine coupled with benevolence and charity."[4]

12. *Ivo.* If that definition satisfies you, I agree that it satisfies me.

13. *Aelred.* In that case, those who have the same opinion, the same will, in matters human and divine, along with mutual benevolence and charity, have, we shall admit, reached the perfection of friendship.

14. *Ivo.* Why not? But still, I do not see what the pagan Cicero meant by the words "charity" and "benevolence."

15. *Aelred.* Perhaps for him the word "charity" expresses an affection of the heart, and the word "benevolence," carrying it out in deed. For mutual harmony itself in matters human and divine ought to be dear to the hearts of both, that is, attractive and precious[5]; and the carrying out of these works in actual practice ought to be both benevolent and pleasant.

16. *Ivo.* I grant that this definition pleases me adequately, except that I should think it applied equally to pagans and Jews, and even to bad Christians. However, I confess that I am convinced that true friendship cannot exist among those who live without Christ.

17. *Aelred.* What follows will make it sufficiently clear to us whether the definition contains too much or too little, so that it may either be rejected, or if, so to say sufficient and not over inclusive, be admitted. You can, however, get some idea of the nature of friendship from the definition, even though it should seem somewhat imperfect.

18. *Ivo.* Please, will I annoy you if I say that this definition does not satisfy me unless you unravel for me the meaning of the word itself?

19. *Aelred.* I shall be glad to comply with your wishes if only you will pardon my lack of knowledge and not force me to teach what I do not know. Now I think the word *amicus* [friend] comes from the word *amor* [love], and *amicitia* [friendship] from *amicus.*[6] For love is a certain "affection" of the rational soul whereby it seeks and eagerly strives after some object to possess it and enjoy it. Having attained its object through love, it enjoys it with a certain interior sweetness, embraces it,

and preserves it. We have explained the affections and movements of love as clearly and carefully as we could in our *Mirror*[7] with which you are already familiar.

20. Furthermore, a friend is called a guardian of love or, as some would have it, a guardian of the spirit itself.[8] Since it is fitting that my friend be a guardian of our mutual love or the guardian of my own spirit so as to preserve all its secrets in faithful silence, let him, as far as he can, cure and endure such defects as he may observe in it; let him rejoice with his friend in his joys, and weep with him in his sorrows,[9] and feel as his own all that his friend experiences.

21. Friendship, therefore, is that virtue by which spirits are bound by ties of love and sweetness, and out of many are made one.[10] Even the philosophers of this world have ranked friendship not with things casual or transitory but with the virtues which are eternal.[11] Solomon in the *Book of Proverbs* appears to agree with them when he says: "He that is a friend loves at all times,"[12] manifestly declaring that friendship is eternal if it is true friendship; but, if it should ever cease to be, then it was not true friendship, even though it seemed to be so.

22. *Ivo.* Why is it, then, that we read about bitter enmities arising between the most devoted friends?[13]

23. *Aelred.* God-willing, we shall discuss that matter more amply in its own place.[14] Meantime remember this: he was never a friend who could offend him whom he at one time received into his friendship; on the other hand, that other has not tasted the delights of true friendship who even when offended has ceased to love him whom he once cherished. For "he that is a friend loves at all times."[15]

24. Although he be accused unjustly, though he be injured, though he be cast in the flames, though he be crucified, "he that is a friend loves at all times."[16] Our Jerome speaks similarly: "A friendship which can cease to be was never true friendship."[17]

Dwelling in Friendship

- Have you ever had a teacher who, like Aelred, taught more through discussion than formal instruction? What are the benefits of such an approach? Do you see any weaknesses in it?

- Does this section of the dialogue reveal anything about Aelred and Ivo's assumptions about the nature of true friendship? In your opinion, do they have any blind spots? Do you have any awareness about what some of your own assumptions regarding friendship might be?

Book One: 25-49

Introduction

W hen Ivo wonders if friendship is even worth striving for, since so much is expected of it (no. 25), Aelred responds by saying that Christians should have great hope in their capacity to share in this virtue (no. 27). Moreover, while the ancient Greeks and Romans could look to only a handful of examples, Christians could boast of thousands of examples of authentic friendships. He points to the countless martyrs who gave their lives for their brothers and sisters, and adds that he could go on citing many more examples (nos. 28-30). When reflecting on the sacrifice of martyrdom, Ivo wonders if any difference exists between charity and friendship (no. 31). Aelred responds that charity is a much wider concept: we are bound to love everyone in charity, even our enemies; we open our hearts in friendship, however, only to those whom we trust and in whom we can confide (no 32).

Ivo then observes that even those leading a worldly existence experience, at times, similar bonds of affection, and he suggests that the discussion would benefit greatly by a clear delineation of the various types of friendship (no. 34). Aelred agrees and says that friendship can be carnal, worldly, or spiritual (no. 38). Carnal friendship seeks nothing but pleasure; it is guided not by reason, but by passion and lust. Such friendships focus on likes and dislikes that incite mutual pleasure and easily come and go (nos. 39-41). Worldly friendship seeks nothing but temporal advantage. It focuses only on a person's usefulness. This kind of friendship ends when either person ceases to be advantageous to the other. It does not endure in times of trouble. Although Aelred admits that it may resemble true friendship somewhat, he insists that its primary concern for temporal advantage prevents it from being authentic (nos. 42-44). Spiritual friendship, by way of contrast, seeks not earthly pleasure or worldly gain, but its own dignity and perfection. It lives by reason and the cardinal virtues. Such a friendship is its own reward. Directed by prudence, ruled by justice, guarded by fortitude, and moderated by temperance, spiritual friends resemble each other in the way they live, in the values they hold, and in the goals they pursue (nos. 45–49).

✣

Text

25. *Ivo.* Since such perfection is expected of true friendship, it is not surprising that those were so rare whom the ancients commended as true friends. As Tullius says: "In so many past ages, tradition extols scarcely three or four pairs of friends."[18] But if in our day, that is, in this age of Christianity, friends are so few, it seems to me that I am exerting myself uselessly in striving after this virtue which I, terrified by its admirable sublimity, now almost despair of ever acquiring.

26. *Aelred.* "Effort in great things," as someone has said, "is itself great."[19] Hence it is the mark of a virtuous mind to reflect continually upon sublime and noble thoughts, that it may either attain the desired object or understand more clearly and gain knowledge of what ought to be desired. Thus, too, he must be supposed to have advanced not a little who has learned, by a knowledge of virtue, how far he is from virtue itself.

27. Indeed, the Christian ought not to despair of acquiring any virtue since daily the divine voice from the Gospel reechoes: "Ask, and you shall receive. . . ."[20] It is no wonder, then, that pursuers of true virtue were rare among the pagans since they did not know the Lord, the Dispenser of virtue,[21] of whom it is written: "The Lord of hosts, he is the King of glory."[22] 28. Indeed, through faith in him they were prepared to die for one another—I do not say three or four, but I offer you thousands of pairs of friends—although the ancients declared or imagined the devotion of Pylades and Orestes a great marvel.[23] Were they not, according to the definition of Tullius, strong in the virtue of true friendship, of whom it is written: "And the multitude of believers had but one heart and one soul; neither did anyone say that aught was his own, but all things were common unto them"?[24] 29. How could they fail to have complete agreement on all things divine and human with charity and benevolence,[25] seeing that they had but one heart

and one soul? How many martyrs gave their lives for their brethren! How many spared neither cost, nor even physical torments! I am sure you have often read—and that not dry-eyed—about the girl of Antioch rescued from a house of ill-repute by a fine bit of strategy on the part of a certain soldier.[26] Sometime later he whom she had discovered as a guardian of her chastity in that house of ill-repute became her companion in martyrdom. 30. I might go on citing many examples of this kind, did not the danger of verboseness forbid, and their very abundance enjoin us to be silent. For Christ Jesus announced their coming. He spoke, and they were multiplied above number.[27] "Greater love than this," he says, "no man has, that a man lay down his life for his friends."[28]

31. *Ivo.* Are we then to believe that there is no difference between charity and friendship?

32. *Aelred.* On the contrary, there is a vast difference; for divine authority approves that more are to be received into the bosom of charity than into the embrace of friendship. For we are compelled by the law of charity to receive in the embrace of love not only our friends but also our enemies.[29] But only those do we call friends to whom we can fearlessly entrust our heart and all its secrets; those, too, who, in turn, are bound to us by the same law of faith and security.

33. *Ivo.* How many persons leading a worldly existence and acting as partners in some form of vice, are united by a similar pact and find the bond of even that sort of friendship to be more pleasant and sweet than all the delights of this world! 34. I hope that you will not find it burdensome to isolate, as it were, from the company of so many types of friendship that one which we think should be called "spiritual" to distinguish it from the others with which it is to some extent bound up and confused and which accost and clamor for the attention of those who seek and long for it. For by contrasting them you would make spiritual friendship better known to us and consequently more desirable, and thus more actively rouse and fire us to its acquisition.

35. *Aelred.* Falsely do they claim the illustrious name of friends among whom there exists a harmony of vices; since he who does not love is not a friend, but he does not love his fellow-man who loves iniquity. "For he that loves iniquity" does not love, but "hates his own soul."[30] Truly, he who does not love his own soul will not be able to love the soul of another.[31] 36. Thus it follows that they glory only in the name of friendship and are deceived by a distorted image and

are not supported by truth. Yet, since such great joy is experienced in friendship which either lust defiles, avarice dishonors, or luxury pollutes, we may infer how much sweetness that friendship possesses which, in proportion as it is nobler, is the more secure; purer, it is the more pleasing; freer, it is the more happy. 37. Let us allow that, because of some similarity in feelings, those friendships which are not true, be, nevertheless, called friendships, provided, however, they are judiciously distinguished from that friendship which is spiritual and therefore true. 38. Hence let one kind of friendship be called carnal, another worldly, and another spiritual. The carnal springs from mutual harmony in vice; the worldly is enkindled by the hope of gain; and the spiritual is cemented by similarity of life, morals, and pursuits among the just.[32]

39. The real beginning of carnal friendship proceeds from an affection which like a harlot directs its step after every passer-by,[33] following its own lustful ears and eyes in every direction.[34] By means of the avenues of these senses it brings into the mind itself images of beautiful bodies or voluptuous objects. To enjoy these as he pleases the carnal man thinks is blessedness, but to enjoy them without an associate he considers less delightful. 40. Then by gesture, nod, words, compliance, spirit is captivated by spirit, and one is inflamed by the other, and they are kindled to form a sinful bond, so that, after they have entered upon such a deplorable pact, the one will do or suffer any crime or sacrilege whatsoever for the sake of the other. They consider nothing sweeter than this type of friendship, they judge nothing more equable, believing community of like and dislike[35] to be imposed upon them by the laws of friendship. 41. And so, this sort of friendship is undertaken without deliberation, is tested by no act of judgment, is in no wise governed by reason; but through the violence of affection is carried away through diverse paths, observing no limit, caring naught for uprightness, foreseeing neither gains nor losses, but advancing toward everything heedlessly, indiscriminately, lightly and immoderately. For that reason, goaded on, as if by furies, it is consumed by its own self, or is dissolved with the same levity with which it was originally fashioned.

42. But worldly friendship, which is born of a desire for temporal advantage or possessions, is always full of deceit and intrigue; it contains nothing certain, nothing constant, nothing secure; for, to be sure, it ever changes with fortune and follows the purse.[36] 43. Hence

it is written: "He is a fair-weather friend, and he will not abide in the day of your trouble."[37] Take away his hope of profit, and immediately he will cease to be a friend. This type of friendship the following lines very aptly deride:

> *A friend, not of the man, but of his purse is he.*
> *Held fast by fortune fair, by evil made to flee.*[38]

44. And yet, the beginning of this vicious friendship leads many individuals to a certain degree of true friendship: those, namely, who at first enter into a compact of friendship in the hope of common profit while they cherish in themselves faith in baneful riches, and who, in so far as human affairs are concerned, reach an acme of pleasing mutual agreement. But a friendship ought in no wise be called true which is begun and preserved for the sake of some temporal advantage.

45. For spiritual friendship, which we call true, should be desired, not for consideration of any worldly advantage or for any extrinsic cause, but from the dignity of its own nature and the feelings of the human heart, so that its fruition and reward is nothing other than itself.[39] 46. Whence the Lord in the Gospel says: "I have appointed you that you should go, and should bring forth fruit,"[40] that is, that you should love one another. For true friendship advances by perfecting itself, and the fruit is derived from feeling the sweetness of that perfection. And so spiritual friendship among the just is born of a similarity in life, morals, and pursuits, that is, it is a mutual conformity in matters human and divine united with benevolence and charity.[41]

47. Indeed, this definition seems to me to be adequate for representing friendship. If, however, "charity" is, according to our way of thinking, named in the sense that friendship excludes every vice, then "benevolence" expresses the feeling to love which is pleasantly roused interiorly. 48. Where such friendship exists, there, indeed, is a community of likes and dislikes,[42] the more pleasant in proportion as it is more sincere, the more agreeable as it is more sacred; those who love in this way can will nothing that is unbecoming, and reject nothing that is expedient. 49. Surely, such friendship prudence directs, justice rules, fortitude guards, and temperance moderates.[43] But of these matters we shall speak in their place. Now, then, tell me whether you think enough has been said about the matter you first brought up, namely, the nature of friendship.

Dwelling in Friendship

- Do you think true friends are hard to find? What does your own experience tell you? Does it coincide with Aelred's perception? Do you agree with him that it is easier for Christians to become friends?

- Does such an opinion hold water today? Is there anything in this section of the treatise that you think needs changing or adapting?

Book One: 50–71

✛

Introduction

When discussing the origins of friendship, Aelred says that the human soul's natural desire for it grows with experience and is confirmed by the sanction of law (no. 51). He asserts that "a certain love for companionship" is naturally found on every level of the hierarchy of being: inanimate creation, animate life, human beings, and angels (nos. 53–57). When focusing on human experience, he cites the biblical account of creation where God says that man should not be alone and so creates woman from the very substance of man (no. 57). In the beginning, he says, nature implanted a desire for both friendship and charity in the human heart. At that time, the two were closely united, and extended freely to everyone (no. 58). Eventually, however, something went terribly awry. Because of the Fall, human desire became corrupted and the two virtues became differentiated: charity alone remained universal in scope; friendship could now involve but a select few (nos. 58–59). Humanity's fall from grace, however, did not extinguish reason completely in the soul; even those who did not live virtuously still felt a need for friendship and society. As a result, the riches, glory, and pleasures of the world meant very little without companions with whom to share them. For this reason, it became necessary for law and precept to distinguish "apparent friends," those who enjoy each other's company for temporal ends, from "true friends," those who are bound together by a love for virtue, especially that of wisdom (nos. 60–61).

When Ivo raises the question of the inconsistency of joining a superior virtue like wisdom with an inferior one like friendship (no. 64), Aelred responds by saying, ". . . very often lesser things are linked with greater, good with better, weaker with stronger" (no. 65). A difference in degree, in his mind, does not exclude the possibility of a connection in some fundamental likeness. He cites the example of chastity in marriage, widowhood, and virginity. These virtues differ in degree, but resemble each other because each is a genuine expression of what it means to live a chaste life (no. 65). In a similar way, friendship may be inferior to wisdom, but resembles it because it too is an authentic expression of charity. Although a lesser virtue, friendship is united to wisdom through charity and, from one perspective, can be considered "nothing else but wisdom" (no. 66). When Ivo questions this conclusion (no. 67), Aelred reminds him that true friendship endures forever only because it is rooted in charity. In a similar way, true friendship cannot be entirely separated from wisdom because each reflects a different degree of eternity, truth, and charity (no. 68). When Ivo asks if we can therefore identify God with friendship (no. 69), Aelred says that although such a statement has no basis in scripture, what is true for charity must in some way also hold for friendship (no. 70). This point, he maintains, will become clearer at a later time when they treat friendship's fruition and usefulness.

Text

50. *Ivo.* Your explanation is certainly sufficient, and nothing else suggests itself to me for further inquiry. But before we go on to other things, I should like to know how friendship first originated among men. Was it by nature, by chance, or by necessity of some kind? Or did it come into practice by some statute or law imposed upon the human race, and did practice then commend it to man?

51. *Aelred.* At first, as I see it, nature itself impressed upon the human soul a desire for friendship, then experience increased that desire, and finally the sanction of the law confirmed it.[44] For God, supremely powerful and supremely good, is sufficient good unto himself, since his good, his joy, his glory, his happiness, is himself.[45]

52. Nor is there anything outside himself which he needs, neither man, nor angel, nor heaven, nor earth, nor anything which these contain. To him every creature proclaims: "You are my God, for you have no need of my goods."[46] Not only is he sufficient unto himself, but he is himself the sufficiency of all things: giving simple being to some, sensation to others, and wisdom over and above these to still others, himself the Cause of all being, the Life of all sensation, the Wisdom of all intelligence.

53. And thus Sovereign Nature has established all natures, has arranged all things in their places, and has discreetly distributed all

things in their own times. He has willed, moreover, for so his eternal reason has directed, that peace encompass all his creatures and society unite them; and thus all creatures obtain from him, who is supremely and purely one, some trace of that unity. For that reason he has left no type of beings alone, but out of many has drawn them together by means of a certain society.

54. Suppose we begin with inanimate creation—what soil or what river produces one single stone of one kind? Or what forest bears but a single tree of a single kind? And so even in inanimate nature a certain love of companionship, so to speak, is apparent, since none of these exists alone but everything is created and thrives in a certain society with its own kind.

And surely in animate life who can easily describe how clear the picture of friendship is, and the image of society and love?[47]

55. And though in all other respects animals are rated irrational, yet they imitate man in this regard to such an extent that we almost believe they act with reason. How they run after one another, play with one another, so express and betray their love by sound and movement, so eagerly and happily do they enjoy their mutual company, that they seem to prize nothing else so much as they do whatever pertains to friendship.[48]

56. For the angels, too, divine Wisdom provided, in that he created not one but many. Among them pleasant companionship and delightful love created the same will, the same desire. Assuredly, since one seemed to be superior, the other inferior, there would have been occasion for envy,[49] had not the charity of friendship prevented it. Their multitude thus excluded solitude, and the bond of charity among many increased their mutual happiness.

57. Finally, when God created man, in order to commend more highly the good of society, he said: "It is not good for man to be alone: let us make him a helper like unto himself."[50] It was from no similar, nor even from the same, material that divine Might formed this help mate, but as a clearer inspiration to charity and friendship he produced the woman from the very substance of the man.[51] How beautiful it is that the second human being was taken from the side of the first, so that nature might teach that human beings are equal and, as it were, collateral, and that there is in human affairs neither a superior nor an inferior, a characteristic of true friendship.

58. Hence, nature from the very beginning implanted the desire for friendship and charity in the heart of man, a desire which an inner sense of affection soon increased with a taste of sweetness. But after the fall of the first man, when with the cooling of charity concupiscence made secret inroads and caused private good to take precedence over the common weal, it corrupted the splendor of friendship and charity through avarice and envy, introducing contentions, emulations, hates and suspicions because the morals of men had been corrupted. 59. From that time the good distinguished between charity and friendship, observing that love ought to be extended even to the hostile and perverse, while no union of will and ideas can exist between the good and wicked. And so friendship which, like charity, was first preserved among all by all, remained according to the natural law among the few good. They saw the sacred laws of faith and society violated by many and bound themselves together by a closer bond of love and friendship. In the midst of the evils which they saw and felt, they rested in the joy of mutual charity. 60. But in those in whom wickedness obliterated every feeling for virtue, reason, which could not be extinguished in them, left the inclination toward friendship and society, so that without companionship riches could hold no charm for the greedy, nor glory for the ambitious, nor pleasure for the sensuous man. There are compacts—even sworn bonds—of union among the wicked which ought to be abhorred. These, clothed with the beautiful name of friendship, ought to have been distinguished from true friendship by law and precept, so that when true friendship was sought, one might not incautiously be ensnared among those other friendships because of some slight resemblance. 61. Thus friendship, which nature has brought into being and practice has strengthened, has by the power of law been regulated. It is evident, then, that friendship is natural, like virtue, wisdom, and the like, which should be sought after and preserved for their own sake as natural goods. Everyone that possesses them makes good use of them, and no one entirely abuses them.[52]

62. *Ivo.* May I ask, do not many people abuse wisdom? Those, I mean, who desire to please men through it, or take pride in themselves by reason of the wisdom placed in them or certainly those who consider it a thing that can be sold, just as they imagine there is a source of revenue in piety.[53]

63. *Aelred.* Our Augustine should satisfy you on that point. Here are his words: "He who pleases himself, pleases a foolish man, because,

to be sure, he is foolish who pleases himself."[54] But the man who is foolish is not wise; and he who is not wise is not wise because he does not possess wisdom. How then does he abuse wisdom who does not even possess it? And so proud chastity is no virtue, because pride itself, which is a vice, makes conformable to itself that which was considered a virtue. Therefore, it is not a virtue, but a vice.

64. *Ivo.* But I tell you, with your forbearance, that it does not seem consistent to me to join wisdom to friendship, since there is no comparison between the two.

65. *Aelred.* In spite of the fact that they are not coequal, very often lesser things are linked with greater, good with better, weaker with stronger. This is particularly true in the case of virtues. Although they vary by reason of a difference in degree, still they are close to one another by reason of similarity. Thus widowhood is near to virginity, conjugal chastity to widowhood. Although there is a great difference between these individual virtues, there is, nevertheless, a conformity in this, that they are virtues. 66. Now, then, conjugal chastity does not fail to be a virtue for the reason that widowhood is superior in continency. And whereas holy virginity is preferred to both, it does not thereby take away the excellence of the others. And yet, if you consider carefully what has been said about friendship, you will find it so close to, even replete with, wisdom, that I might almost say friendship is nothing else but wisdom.

67. *Ivo.* I am amazed, I admit, but I do not think that I can easily be convinced of your view.

68. *Aelred.* Have you forgotten that Scripture says: "He that is a friend loves at all times"?[55] Our Jerome also, as you recall, says: "Friendship which can end was never true friendship."[56] That friendship cannot even endure without charity has been more than adequately established. Since then in friendship eternity blossoms, truth shines forth, and charity grows sweet, consider whether you ought to separate the name of wisdom from these three.

69. *Ivo.* What does this all add up to? Shall I say of friendship what John, the friend of Jesus, says of charity: "God is friendship"?[57]

70. *Aelred.* That would be unusual, to be sure, nor does it have the sanction of the Scriptures. But still what is true of charity, I surely do not hesitate to grant to friendship, since "he that abides in friendship, abides in God, and God in him."[58] That we shall see more clearly when we begin to discuss its fruition and utility. Now if we have said enough

on the nature of friendship in view of the simplicity of our poor wit, let us reserve for another time the other points you proposed for solution.

71. *Ivo.* I admit that my eagerness finds such a delay quite annoying, but it is necessary since not only is it time for the evening meal, from which no one may be absent, but, in addition, there are the burdensome demands of the other religious who have a right to your care.

Dwelling in Friendship

- Does Book One come to a natural conclusion? What points raised by Ivo earlier in the treatise have not yet been discussed? Has Aelred and Ivo's conversation raised any questions or doubts in your own mind about the nature of friendship? If so, can you think of anyone with whom you can discuss them? With whom do you discuss your serious concerns about the spiritual life?

Book One Review

- Do you believe that true friendship must be rooted in Christ? If so, in what way? Must Christ's presence be consciously acknowledged in the friendship? Is it possible for a true friendship to exist without each person being conscious of Christ's presence in his or her life? What does Aelred say about friendships among non-Christians? Do you agree with him? What do you believe about the nature of true friendship?

- Do you agree with the way Aelred describes the relationship between charity and friendship? What do you like about it? Is there anything you disagree with? Do you think Aelred's description is an accurate representation of their relationship? In what ways are charity and friendship similar? In what ways are they different? Toward which do you feel more drawn? Can you explain why?

- Do you agree with Aelred's description of carnal, worldly, and spiritual friendships? Has he omitted anything? Is there anything you would add or subtract? Have you experienced any friendships that Aelred would describe as carnal or worldly? Have you experienced any that Aelred would describe as spiritual? Do you think that Aelred expects too much from spiritual friendship? Is it possible for genuine friendships to have elements of all three types? If so, how? Can Aelred's presentation be adapted to include such a possibility?

- Do you agree with Aelred's distinction between apparent friendship and true friendship? Do these friendships have any specific traits or characteristics that might help you distinguish them from one another? What image or metaphor would you use to describe the difference between them? What roles do law and precept play in distinguishing them? Have you ever mistaken an apparent friendship for a true one? Have you ever mistaken a true friendship for an apparent one? Is it possible for an apparent friendship to develop into a true friendship?

- How would you describe Aelred's understanding of humanity's fall? Do you agree with it? How does it fit into his presentation of the relationship between charity and friendship? How does it fit in with his presentation of the various types of friendship? How does it fit in with his presentation of the origin of friendship? How does it fit in with his presentation of the need for the sanction of law? To what extent is the doctrine of the Fall essential to Aelred's understanding of spiritual friendship? Can you explain as much as Aelred does without it?

Book Two

The Fruition and Excellence of Friendship

Book Two: An Overview

A elred emphasizes a number of important new themes in Book Two. For one thing, he increases the number of people involved in the dialogue from two to three. Walter and Gratian, two monks with deep spiritual hungers and highly inquisitive minds, have become Aelred's new dialogue partners. The conversation on friendship resumes because of Walter's desire to read the recently discovered manuscript of Aelred's prior dialogue with his late friend, Ivo. This simple setting for the book shows that spiritual friendship is a perennial concern in life and, as Aelred's warm words about Ivo indicate, is a bond that lingers after death. It also reminds us that spiritual friendship should not be cliquish and closed in upon itself, but open to forging new bonds in an ever-widening circle of fellowship. When seen in this light, Aelred's friendship with Walter and Gratian does not replace the one he shares with Ivo, but deepens his understanding of what friendship in Christ truly means.

Aelred also emphasizes friendship's capacity to move us forward in the spiritual life by helping us to establish an intimate relationship with God. Such a relationship, he maintains, is essential for happiness in both this life and the next. Without such companionship, nothing in this world can ever be truly enjoyed. Such an insight brings an eschatological, "already-but-not-yet" quality to the treatise. True spiritual friends enjoy the bond they share during their sojourn through life, but look forward to its fullest maturation in the next. As a spiritual friendship deepens, Christ, the invisible partner of Book One, emerges from the background and gradually becomes the central focus of concern. Ivo's departure from this life heightens Aelred's awareness of the destiny of all who celebrate, enjoy, and share in the close spiritual bond that comes with friendship in Christ. We almost sense that, along with Christ, Ivo has also become a silent partner in the conversation that Aelred resumes in Book Two with Walter and Gratian.

It is also important to take note of the spirited monastic humor that Aelred weaves into his dialogue through the comic exchanges between Walter and Gratian. This light humor comes out in playful jesting and comic "turns of phrase," and reminds us that spiritual friendship encourages a healthy, childlike playfulness in our relations with others. True friends meet each other on many levels, and are not always serious in their comportment and demeanor. That Aelred, Walter, and Gratian are able to enjoy each other's company and even joke with each other while engaging in a serious discussion says something about the quality and depth of the bond they share. Although they are careful not to allow their playfulness to get out of hand, or to deteriorate into silliness or inappropriate criticism, they are able through their healthy good humor to celebrate the warp and woof of daily life. Spiritual friendship is not a matter of studying and theorizing, but of celebrating and sharing. Aelred most likely includes this important human quality because of his own experience of friendship. He may even have chosen the dialogue form because it lends itself particularly well to expressing this elusive but nonetheless important experiential aspect of friendship. As a Cistercian monk, Aelred is much more interested in experience than in theory, especially when it comes to something so important for growth in the spiritual life.

On another note, Aelred's metaphor of the "threefold kiss"—the corporeal, spiritual, and intellectual—heightens the experiential dimensions of the treatise and offers a very concrete symbol for understanding what happens to people who become friends with one another and with God. For Aelred, this threefold kiss represents a movement from the physical to the spiritual to the mystical. To understand him, it is important to recognize that Aelred believes that reality is ordered in a hierarchical fashion, and has both visible and invisible dimensions to it. He also considers the human person a microcosm of all that the universe holds.

On the physical level, perhaps nothing is more beautiful than the exchange of breath that takes place between two people in love. Inspired by the first verse of the *Song of Songs* (1:1), Aelred applies the metaphor of the kiss both to spiritual friendship and to friendship with God. A spiritual kiss occurs when two people enter into spiritual friendship, and their spirits mingle and touch in a free exchange of spiritual breath. An intellectual (or better yet, "divine" or "mystical") kiss occurs when a person's spirit mingles with and touches the Spirit of God in a free exchange of life-giving grace. The carnal kiss, for Aelred, is but a faint reflection of the spiritual kiss which, in turn, is but a faint reflection of the intellectual. While all three are important on their respective levels, they should not be mistaken for one another or confused in any way.

Aelred's understanding of what it means to be "good" is also very important in the discussion. In his mind, only good people can be friends. Such a statement, however, should not discourage ordinary people, but actually encourage them to pursue such relationships. For Aelred, a "good person" is not someone who is perfect and without fault, but one who is leading a life of conversion. A "good person" is not so much a saint, but someone who wishes to be a saint. Spiritual friendship, in Aelred's mind, was made for such people and is an important instrument for helping them reach their goal.

It is also important to note that Aelred's discussion of the three types of friendship (i.e., puerile, advantageous, and spiritual) began earlier in Book One, and flows from his distinction between apparent and true friendship. Apparent friendships may seem to be true, but seek only pleasure or some other personal advantage. True friendship is its own justification, and is motivated by a desire for the good of the other. Although true friends do in fact bring pleasure and advantage to each other, their primary focus is always the other's well-being. True friends refuse to pursue anything that will lead to the death of the soul.

Finally, it is clear from the dialogue that Aelred's ideas on friendship flow from his own personal experience. His discussion with Walter and Gratian is a reflection of his own deep internal dialogue about what it really means to befriend another in Christ. We should read Book Two with an eye to this process of personal discovery and continual conversion. It makes little sense to read, if reading it does not help us to forge close bonds with others and with Christ. Discussing the practical advantages, the limitations, and the fruits of spiritual friendship has little value if it does not encourage us to reflect upon the quality of relationships in our own lives, and to ask ourselves if they are a help or a hindrance in fostering our relationship with God.

Book Two: 1–7

Introduction

Book Two takes place long after the death of Aelred's friend Ivo. The circle of conversation has widened from two to three persons and now involves Aelred and two younger monks of the monastery, Walter and Gratian.

The book opens with a brief encounter between Aelred and Walter, who was impatiently sitting apart from everyone, while his abbot was conducting business affairs with some people from beyond the monastery walls (no. 1). Walter's impatience stems from his inability to have time to speak with Aelred about spiritual concerns (no. 2). Aelred tells Walter that this spiritual hunger will help him to appreciate even more the time they now have at their disposal (no. 3). When asked what he would like to discuss, Walter responds that he would like to study the recently discovered document containing Aelred's conversation with Ivo about the nature of spiritual friendship to see if anything in it needs further discussion (nos. 4, 6). Aelred agrees to let Walter read the document, but cautions him to read it privately and not draw attention to it, since he may still wish to revise it at some future date (no. 7).

Text

1. *Aelred.* Come here now, brother, and tell me why you were sitting all alone a little while ago at some distance from us, when I was dealing with material affairs with those men of the flesh. There you were, turning your eyes now this way, now that; then you would rub your forehead with your hand; presently you would run your fingers through your hair;[1] again, frowning angrily, you would, with all sorts

---

of faces, complain that something quite apart from your own desires had happened to you.

2. *Walter.* You have described the situation perfectly. For who could preserve his patience through a whole day seeing those agents of Pharaoh[2] getting your full attention, while we, to whom you are particularly indebted, were not able to gain even so much as a word with you?

3. *Aelred.* But we must show kindness to such people, too, for either we expect benefits from them or we fear their enmity. But since the doors have finally been closed upon them, solitude is the more gratifying to me now, in proportion as that preceding disturbance was distressing. You know, "the best appetizer is hunger"[3]; and neither honey nor any other spice gives such relish to wine as a strong thirst does to water. And so perhaps this conference of ours, like spiritual food and drink, will be more enjoyable to you because of the intense longing preceding it. Come now, and do not delay proposing to me what you were preparing to unravel from your troubled heart a little while ago.

4. *Walter.* I shall, indeed; for if I be minded to make excuses because of the time, I shall be making even shorter the brief period they have left us. Tell me now, please, has it escaped your mind, or do you still remember the conversation which, once upon a time, you and your friend Ivo had on spiritual friendship? Do you recall what questions he proposed to you, how far you advanced in the explanation of these, and what you set down in writing upon the same points?

5. *Aelred.* Indeed, the fond memory of my beloved Ivo, yes, his constant love and affection are, in fact, always so fresh to my mind, that, though he has gone from this life in body, yet to my spirit he seems never to have died at all. For there he is ever with me,[4] there his pious countenance inspires me, there his charming eyes smile upon me, there his happy words have such relish for me, that either I seem to have gone to a better land with him or he seems still to be dwelling with me here upon earth. But you know that very many years have passed since we lost that bit of paper on which I had written his questions and my answers on spiritual friendship.

6. *Walter.* The facts do not escape me, but to be candid, all my eagerness and impatience arises from the fact that I have heard from certain individuals that this very paper was found and handed over to you three days ago. Please, show it to your son, for my spirit will not rest until I have reviewed the whole discussion and see what is still wanting

in it, and then present to your fatherly examination for rejection or acceptance or explanation whatever my own mind or secret inspiration suggest to me as matters requiring discussion.

7. *Aelred.* I shall comply with your wishes, but I desire that you alone should read what is written on it, and that it be not brought to public attention.[5] For I may, perhaps, decide that some points are to be omitted, some added, and, surely, many to be corrected.

Dwelling in Friendship

- Does the opening setting of Book Two in any way resemble that of Book One? Are there any clear differences? What are the similarities and dissimilarities in temperament between Walter and Ivo? Do you think they were real persons or fictitious characters created by Aelred for purposes of the dialogue? Could they share aspects of both? Does Aelred's description of his friendship with Ivo come across as authentic? Have you ever felt that way about anyone?

Book Two: 8–27

✛

Introduction

At this point, a change of scene takes place. Some time has passed, and Walter has had time to examine Aelred's dialogue with Ivo. He tells Aelred that he enjoyed what he read, but would now like to know about the practical advantages of spiritual friendship for those who foster it (no. 8). Aelred replies that friendship bears fruit in both this life and the next. Nothing is more sacred, more useful, more difficult to find, more pleasant, and more profitable than true friendship. Without authentic spiritual friendship, it is next to impossible to be happy in this life. A person without friends is more like a beast than a human being. Spiritual friendship, he maintains, cultivates virtue, overcomes vice, and brings balance in both good times and bad. It is a medicine for life that heals and elevates. As such, it leads one to the love and knowledge of God (nos. 9–14).

Walter is clearly moved by Aelred's description of spiritual friendship and wishes to hear more (no. 15). At this point, Gratian, another monk of the monastery, comes along and joins in the conversation. This young monk brings some comic relief to the dialogue. Walter jokes with him by calling him "friendship's child" for putting so much energy into loving and being loved (no. 16). Gratian thanks Walter for the compliment, but wonders why he was not invited to share in the discussion earlier if those were Walter's true sentiments. Aelred eases Gratian's concern that he has missed a number of important points (no. 17) by telling him that they have barely begun and still have much to discuss (no. 18).

He goes on to say that spiritual friends share in Christ's heart and soul (no. 21). He likens the various stages of friendship to a threefold kiss: the carnal, the spiritual, and the intellectual (no. 24). All three involve an exchange of breath. The first occurs through the touch of lips; the second, through the union of spirits; the third, through union with the Spirit of God and the infusion of divine grace. The corporeal kiss, Aelred maintains, should be given sparingly and only with good reason, such as when reconciling another or giving someone a sign of peace. He cautions against misusing it for shameful purposes (nos. 24–25). The spiritual kiss, he claims, occurs when two people become close friends and experience a mingling of their spirits (no. 26). The intellectual kiss, by way of contrast, occurs when someone becomes a friend of God and the Holy Spirit touches his or her spirit in an intimate encounter (no. 27).

✤

Text

8.	*Walter.* Look, here I am, all ears to take in every word, the more avidly so since what I have read on friendship has so pleasant a taste. Since, therefore, I have read this excellent discussion on the nature of friendship, I should like to have you tell me what practical advantages it procures for those who cultivate it. For though it is a matter of such moment, as you seem to have thoroughly proved by means of unassailable arguments, yet it is only when its purpose and benefit are understood that it will be sought after with genuine ardor.

9. *Aelred.* I do not presume that I can explain it in a manner befitting the dignity of so signal a good, since in human affairs nothing more sacred is striven for, nothing more useful is sought after, nothing more difficult is discovered, nothing more sweet experienced, and nothing more profitable possessed. For friendship bears fruit in this life and in the next.[6]

10. It manifests all the virtues by its own charms; it assails vices by its own virtue; it tempers adversity and moderates prosperity. As a result, scarcely any happiness whatever can exist among mankind without friendship,[7] and a man is to be compared to a beast if he has no one to rejoice with him in adversity, no one to whom to unburden his mind if any annoyance crosses his path or with whom to share some unusually sublime or illuminating inspiration.[8] 11. "Woe to him that is alone, for when he falls, he has none to lift him up."[9] He is entirely alone who is without a friend.

But what happiness, what security, what joy to have someone to whom you dare to speak on terms of equality as to another self;[10] one to whom you need have no fear to confess your failings; one to whom you can unblushingly make known what progress you have made in the spiritual life; one to whom you can entrust all the secrets of your heart and before whom you can place all your plans! What, therefore, is more pleasant than so to unite to oneself the spirit of another and of two to form one, that no boasting is thereafter to be feared, no suspicion to be dreaded, no correction of one by the other to cause pain, no praise on the part of one to bring a charge of adulation from the other. 12. "A friend," says the Wise Man, "is the medicine of life."[11] Excellent, indeed, is that saying. For medicine is not more powerful or more efficacious for our wounds in all our temporal needs than the possession of a friend who meets every misfortune joyfully, so that, as the Apostle says, shoulder to shoulder, they bear one another's burdens.[12] Even more—each one carries his own injuries even more lightly than that of his friend. 13. Friendship, therefore, heightens the joys of prosperity and mitigates the sorrows of adversity by dividing and sharing them.[13] Hence, the best medicine in life is a friend. Even the philosophers took pleasure in the thought: not even water, nor the sun, nor fire do we use in more instances than a friend.[14] In every action, in every pursuit, in certainty, in doubt, in every event and fortune of whatever sort, in private and in public, in every deliberation, at home and abroad, everywhere friendship is found to be appreciated, a friend a necessity, a friend's service a thing of utility. "Wherefore, friends," says Tullius, "though absent are present, though poor are rich, though weak are strong, and—what seems stranger still—though dead are alive.[15] 14. And so it is that the rich prize friendship as their glory, the exiles as their native land, the poor as their wealth, the sick as their medicine, the dead as their life, the healthy as their charm, the weak as their strength and the strong as their prize. So great are the distinction, memory, praise, and affection that accompany friends that their lives are adjudged worthy of praise and their death rated as precious.[16] And, a thing even more excellent than all these considerations, friendship is a stage bordering upon that perfection which consists in the love and knowledge of God, so that man from being a friend of his fellowman becomes the friend of God, according to the words of the Savior in the Gospel: "I will not now call you servants, but my friends."[17]

15. *Walter.* I confess your words have so moved me and so enkindled my soul to a burning desire for friendship, that I believe I am not even alive as long as I am deprived of the manifold benefits of this great good. But what you said last, the statement which aroused me so completely and almost carried me away from all earthly things, I desire

to hear developed more fully, namely, that among the stages leading to perfection friendship is the highest.

16. But see, here comes our friend Gratian, and quite opportunely. I might rightly call him friendship's child for he spends all his energy in seeking to be loved and to love.[18] It is opportune he came along, since he might be too eager for friendship and be deceived by its mere semblance, mistake the counterfeit for the true, the imaginary for the real, the carnal for the spiritual.

17. *Gratian.*[19] I thank you for your courtesy, brother. One not invited but rather boldly imposing himself, you grant a place at this spiritual banquet. But if you thought that I should be called friendship's child in earnest and not in jest, I should have been sent for at the beginning of this talk, and then I would not have had to lay aside due modesty and make a display of my eagerness. Nevertheless, Father, continue where you began, and for my sake set something on the table, so that, if I cannot be satiated as he is (for after consuming I know not how many courses, he summons me now to the remnants of the banquet of which he has grown disdainful), I may at least be able to be refreshed a little.

18. *Aelred.* You need have no fear, son, since matters of such importance still remain to be said on the good of friendship that, if some wise person were to carry them through to the end, you would think we had thus far said nothing. Nevertheless, turn your attention briefly to the manner in which friendship is, so to say, a stage toward the love and knowledge of God. Indeed, in friendship there is nothing dishonorable, nothing deceptive, nothing feigned; whatever there is, is holy, voluntary, and true.[20] And this itself is also a characteristic of charity.[21] 19. In this, truly, friendship shines forth with a special right of its own, that among those who are bound by the tie of friendship, all joys, all security, all sweetness, all charms are experienced. Therefore, in the perfection of charity we love very many who are a source of burden and grief to us, for whose interest we concern ourselves honorably, not with hypocrisy or dissimulation, but sincerely and voluntarily, but yet we do not admit these to the intimacy of our friendship. 20. And so in friendship are joined honor and charm, truth and joy, sweetness and good will, affection and action. And all these take their beginning from Christ, advance through Christ, and are perfected in Christ. Therefore, not too steep or unnatural does the ascent appear from Christ, as the inspiration of the love by which we love our friend, to Christ giving

himself to us as our Friend for us to love, so that charm may follow upon charm, sweetness upon sweetness and affection upon affection. 21. And thus, friend cleaving to friend in the spirit of Christ, is made with Christ but one heart and one soul,[22] and so mounting aloft through degrees of love to friendship with Christ, he is made one spirit with him in one kiss.[23] Aspiring to this kiss the saintly soul cries out: "Let him kiss me with the kiss of his mouth."[24]

22. Let us consider the character of that carnal kiss, so that we may pass from the carnal to the spiritual, from the human to the divine.[25] Man needs two elements to sustain life, food and air. Without food he can subsist for some time, but without air he cannot live even one hour. And so in order to live, we inhale air with our mouths and exhale it. And that very thing which we exhale or inhale we call breath. 23. Therefore, in a kiss two breaths meet, and are mingled, and are united. As a result, a certain sweetness of mind is born, which rouses and binds together the affection of those who embrace.[26]

24. There is, then, a corporeal kiss, a spiritual kiss, and an intellectual kiss. The corporeal kiss is made by the impression of the lips; the spiritual kiss by the union of spirits; the intellectual kiss through the Spirit of God, by the infusion of grace.

Now the corporeal kiss ought not to be offered or received except for definite and worthy reasons: for example, as a sign of reconciliation, when they become friends who were previously at enmity with one another;[27] or as a mark of peace, as those who are about to communicate in church manifest by an external kiss their interior peace; or as a symbol of love, such as is permitted between bride and bridegroom or as is extended to and received from friends after a long absence; or as a sign of catholic unity, as is done when a guest is received. 25. But just as many people misuse water, fire, iron, food, and air, which are natural goods, by employing them as instruments of their cruelty and lust, so, too, the perverse and lustful strive to give a relish to their shameful acts even with this good which the natural law has instituted to signify the things we have indicated, defiling this very kiss with such shame that thus to be kissed is nothing else than to be corrupted. How much such a kiss ought to be detested, abominated, shunned, resisted, every honorable person knows.

26. In the next place, the spiritual kiss is characteristically the kiss of friends who are bound by one law of friendship; for it is not made by contact of the mouth but by the affection of the heart;[28] not by

a meeting of lips but by a mingling of spirits, by the purification of all things in the Spirit of God,[29] and, through his own participation, it emits a celestial savor. I would call this the kiss of Christ, yet he himself does not offer it from his own mouth, but from the mouth of another,[30] breathing upon his lovers that most sacred affection so that there seems to them to be, as it were, one spirit in many bodies. And they may say with the Prophet: "Behold how good and how pleasant it is for brethren to dwell together in unity."[31] 27. The soul, therefore, accustomed to this kiss and not doubting that all this sweetness comes from Christ, as if reflecting within itself and saying, "Oh, if only he himself had come!" sighs for the kiss of grace and with the greatest desire exclaims: "Let him kiss me with the kiss of his mouth."[32] So that now, after all earthly affections have been tempered, and all thoughts and desires which savor of the world have been quieted, the soul takes delight in the kiss of Christ alone and rests in his embrace, exulting and exclaiming: "His left hand is under my head and his right hand shall embrace me."[33]

Dwelling in Friendship

- Does Gratian's arrival on the scene change the course of the conversation in any way? What does he bring to the discussion? Does he detract from it? Does he move it forward? How would you describe his relationship with Walter and Aelred? Why does Aelred decide to introduce another dialogue partner relatively early on in Book Two? Just how wide should our circle of friendship extend?

Book Two: 28–53

✥

Introduction

At this point, Gratian remarks that the last kind of friendship, that which culminates in friendship with God, must be very rare and seems to run counter to his common understanding of friendship as a simple harmony of wills (no. 26). Walter, in turn, wonders about the limits of friendship and asks Aelred for some insight into the practical boundaries of what one should and should not do for a friend (nos. 29–30). He jokes by saying that he asks this question primarily for Gratian's benefit (no. 31), and Gratian responds by telling Walter that he would prefer to hear what Aelred has to say before responding in kind (no. 32).

According to Aelred, the limit of true friendship was set forth by Christ when he said there is no greater love than to lay down one's life for one's friends (no. 33). Gratian agrees that this is an adequate description of the limits of friendship (no. 34), but Walter insists that sinners and unbelievers are sometimes willing to lay down their lives for each other to achieve evil purposes (no. 35). Aelred replies that only the good can be true friends. He says that friendship begins with the good, progresses with the better, and reaches its completion with the perfect. Friendship, by its very nature, does not delight in evil. He cites numerous examples from scripture and Church history to support his claim (nos. 36, 38–41).

If this is so, then Gratian wonders if friendship is an impossible goal for most ordinary people, since it concerns only the good (no. 42). Aelred replies that by "good" he does not mean someone who is entirely without fault or imperfection, but only one who tries to live in a sober, just, and godly way (no. 43). After listening to Aelred, Walter wonders if one should avoid friendship altogether, because it means getting involved in another person's life and is sure to bring much grief and many burdens (nos. 45–46). Gratian disagrees with Walter (no. 47), and the two young monks look to Aelred for counsel (no. 48).

At this point, Aelred points to Cicero, the Apostle Paul, and the friendship between Chusai the Arachite and King David to reiterate his claim that those without friends resemble beasts more than human beings (nos. 49–53).

✣

Text

28. *Gratian.* This type of friendship, as I see it, is not common, nor are we accustomed to dream of friendship as having such a character. I do not know what thought Walter has given it so far, but, as for me, I believed friendship was nothing else than so complete an identity of wills between two persons that the one would wish nothing which the other did not wish,[34] and that so great was the mutual harmony between both, in fortune good and evil, that neither life, nor wealth, nor honor, nothing whatsoever belonging to the one was denied to the other for his enjoyment and use according as he wished.

29. *Walter.* I remember having learned something quite different in the first dialogue where the very definition of friendship, set forth and explained, duly and ardently inspired me to a more profound contemplation of its fruit. As we have been sufficiently informed on this point, we are trying to set up for ourselves a definite limit as to how far friendship ought to go, since in this matter there is a difference of opinion among various individuals. Now there are some who think they ought to love their friends contrary to faith and honor, contrary to common or private good. Some judge that faith alone excepted, the rest should not be held back.[35] 30. Others believe that on behalf of a friend one ought to spurn money, reject honors, submit to enmities from those in high places, and not even shun exile; that one should even expose oneself to what is dishonorable and vile, provided only one's native land is not the sufferer nor one's neighbor hurt. Again there are those who set up this as the goal of friendship, that each one will so conduct himself toward his friend as he would toward himself. 31. And some believe they satisfy the demands of friendship when they mutually repay their friend for every benefit of service.[36]

But from this discussion of ours, I am convinced that I ought not have faith in any of these theorists, and for that reason I should like you to set up a definite limit for friendship, particularly on account of Gratian here, that he may not, in accordance with his name, be so eager to be gracious that he recklessly become vicious.

32. *Gratian.* I sincerely appreciate your thoughtful concern for me; and if I were not hampered by my eagerness to hear, I should, perhaps, take my revenge on you now. But let us hear together what response he plans to give to your questioning.

33. *Aelred.* Christ himself set up a definite goal for friendship when he said: "Greater love than this no man hath, that a man lay down his life for his friends."[37] See how far love between friends should extend; namely, that they be willing to die for one another. Does that seem adequate to you?

34. *Gratian.* Since no greater friendship is possible, why should it not be adequate?

35. *Walter.* But if the wicked or pagans take such joy in the mutual harmony of evil and wickedness that they are willing to die for one another, shall we grant that they have reached the zenith of friendship?

36. *Aelred.* Heaven forbid, since friendship cannot exist among the wicked.

37. *Gratian.* Tell us, pray, among whom it can arise and be preserved?

38. *Aelred.* I shall tell you in a few words. It can begin among the good, progress among the better, and be consummated among the perfect.[38] For as long as any one delights in an evil thing from a desire of evil, as long as sensuality is more gratifying than purity, indiscretion than moderation, flattery than correction, how can it be right for such a one even to aspire to friendship, when it springs from an esteem for virtue?[39] It is difficult therefore, nay, impossible, for you to taste its beginnings, if you do not know the fountain from which it can spring.

39. For that love is shameful and unworthy of the name of friendship wherein anything foul is demanded of a friend; and this is precisely what one is forced to do, if, with vices in no wise dormant or subdued, he is either enticed or impelled to all sorts of illicit acts. Therefore, one ought to detest the opinion of those who think that one should act in behalf of a friend in a way detrimental to faith and uprightness. 40. For it is not excuse for sin, that you sin for the sake of a friend.

The first of men, Adam, would have done better had he charged his wife with presumption instead of complying with her request by eating the forbidden fruit.[40] And far better did the servants of King Saul preserve their loyalty to their master by withdrawing their hands from blood in violation of his command, than Doeg, the Edomite, who as minister of the royal cruelty killed with sacrilegious hands the priests of the Lord.[41] Jonadab, too, the friend of Ammon, would have acted more laudably in preventing the incest of his friend than by offering advice to aid him in obtaining his object.[42] 41. Nor does the virtue of friendship excuse the friends of Absalom, who, consenting to treason, bore arms against their native country.[43] But to come to these our own times, Otto, Cardinal of the Roman Church, certainly was far more blessed in abandoning his close friend Guido than John was in clinging to his Octavian in so great a schism.[44] You see, therefore, that friendship cannot exist except among the good.[45]

42. *Gratian.* What, then, has friendship to do with us, who are not good?

43. *Aelred.* I am not cutting "good" so finely as do some who call no one "good" unless he is lacking no whit in perfection. [46] We call a man "good" who, according to the limits of our mortality,[47] "living soberly and justly and godly in this world,"[48] is resolved neither to ask others to do wrong nor to do wrong himself at another's request.[49] Among such, indeed, we do not doubt that friendship can spring up and that by such it can be perfected. 44. As for those who, apart from faith, danger to their fatherland, or unjust injury to another, put themselves at the disposal of the pleasure of their friends, I would say they are not so foolish as they are insane; sparing others, they do not see fit to spare themselves; and safeguarding the honor of others they unhappily betray their own.[50]

45. *Walter.* I almost agree with the opinion of those who say that friendship should be avoided, on the ground that it is a compact full of solicitude and care, not devoid of fear, and even subject to many griefs.[51] For since it is enough and more than enough for anyone to bear his own burden,[52] they say a man acts rashly in so tying himself to others, that he must needs be involved in many cares and afflicted with many evils. 46. Moreover, they think nothing is more difficult than for friendship to abide even to the day of death, while on the other hand it would be quite shameful for a friendship to be formed and then turn into the opposite.[53] Therefore they judge it safer so to love others as to be able to hate them at will, and in so relaxed a manner to hold the reins of friendship that they may be tightened or loosened at will.[54]

47. *Gratian.* We have been laboring in vain, then, you in speaking, we in listening, if we can so easily withhold ourselves from the desire of friendship, the fruit of which is so holy, so useful, so acceptable to God, and so near to perfection and recommended to us in so many ways. Let us leave the opinion you have spoken of to the man who wishes today's love to be such that it may turn into hatred tomorrow; who wishes to be the friend of all without trusting any; who praises today and reviles tomorrow; who flatters today and criticizes tomorrow; who today is prepared for kisses and tomorrow is ready for reproaches. The love of such a man is acquired at a small price, and at the slightest offense it disappears.

48. *Walter.* I used to think that doves lacked gall. But at any rate tell us how the opinion of those individuals who displease Gratian so much can be refuted.

49. *Aelred.* Tullius speaks beautifully on this point: "They seem," he says, "to take the sun out of the world who take friendship out of life, for we have nothing better from God, nothing more pleasant."[55] What wisdom is there in despising friendship so that you may avoid solicitude, be free from cares, be devoid of fear?—as if any virtue can be acquired or preserved without solicitude.[56] Take your own life—does prudence struggle against error, temperance against wantonness, justice against cunning, fortitude against cowardice, without any great anxiety on your part? 50. Who, I ask, among men, especially among the young, is able to preserve his purity or restrain his sensual appetite without very great grief or fear?

Paul must have been a fool, for he was unwilling to live without care and solicitude for others; but for the sake of charity which he believed to be the sovereign virtue, he was weak with the weak, on fire with the scandalized.[57] And too, great sorrow was his and continual grief of heart on behalf of his brethren in the flesh.[58] 51. Therefore he ought to have given up charity, assuredly under so many anxieties and griefs, now being "against labor" for those whom he had begotten;[59] now "cherishing as a nurse"[60]; now as a master admonishing[61]; now fearing lest their minds be seduced from the faith[62]; now with much grief and many tears exhorting to penance[63]; now grieving over the impenitent.[64]

You see how those seek to take virtues out of the world who fear not to take solicitude, their associate, from our midst. 52. Was it to no purpose that Chusai, the Arachite, preserved with such great fidelity his friendship with David, that he preferred anxiety, and would rather share the griefs of his friend than relax amid the joys and honors of the parricide?[65] I would say that those men are beasts rather than human beings who declare that a man ought to live in such a way as to be to no one a source of consolation, to no one a source even of grief or burden; to take no delight in the good fortune of another, or impart to others no bitterness because of their own misfortune, caring to cherish no one and to be cherished by no one. 53. Heaven forbid that I should grant that they truly love anyone who think of friendship as a trade; for such with their lips only declare themselves friends when the hope of some temporal advantage favors them or when they try to make their friend an accomplice in some sort of base deed.[66]

Dwelling in Friendship

- Are Aelred, Walter, and Gratian relating to each other as equals in this section of the dialogue? Although Aelred is clearly the more learned of the three and, as abbot, has a position of authority over the others, does he treat them with dignity and respect? Does he freely descend to their level? Does he raise them to his? Does their conversation seem genuine and heartfelt or superficial and contrived?

Book Two: 54–72

✤

Introduction

Aelred goes on to point out that one must distinguish between true friendship and the mere semblance of friendship (no. 54). He is firm in his belief that friendship cannot last except among the good, and that those who actively seek what is unbecoming cannot be true friends (no. 55). When asked by Gratian how one determines what is becoming and unbecoming in friendship (no. 56), Aelred responds by distinguishing between puerile friendships, friendships of advantage, and spiritual friendships. A puerile friendship is aimless, based on pleasure, and ruled by the affections. It is rooted in concupiscence and the desires of the flesh (nos. 57–59). A friendship of advantage focuses on a person's usefulness. Its primary purpose is to make some use of the other person for one's own benefit and is not genuinely interested in the other person's well-being (nos. 60-61). A spiritual friendship desires the good of the other person. It is moderate, based on reason, and of pure intention. Such a friendship is well ordered, a delight to experience, and its own reward. It leads a person to divine contemplation and readies him or her to be befriended by God (nos. 59, 62).

Aelred concludes with some examples from scripture to support his claims (nos. 62–64), as well as a summary of all the ground that he has covered in the course of their conversation (nos. 64, 66–69). When Gratian asks him to develop further the limits and cautions one should have when serving one's friend (no. 70), Aelred says that such matters still need to be discussed, but must wait for another day because an hour has already passed and he has other matters to attend to (no. 71). Walter grudgingly agrees, but vows to seek him out the next day at an opportune time (no. 72).

✤

Text

54. *Walter.* Since, therefore, it is agreed that many are deceived by the mere semblance of friendship, tell us, pray, what sort of friendship we ought to avoid and what sort we ought to seek, cherish and preserve.

55. *Aelred.* Since we have said that friendship cannot endure except among the good, it is easy for you to see that no friendship which would be unbecoming to the good is acceptable.

56. *Gratian.* But perhaps we are not clear on the distinction between what is becoming and what is unbecoming.

57. *Aelred.* I shall comply with your wishes and state in a few words what friendships ought to be avoided should they present themselves to us. There is the puerile friendship begotten of an aimless and playful affection, directing its step after every passer-by without reason, without weight, without measure, without consideration of advantage or disadvantage. This type of friendship for a time affects one strongly, it draws one rather closely, and entices one rather flatteringly. But affection without reason is an animal movement, inclined to everything illicit, nay, unable to discern licit from illicit.[67] Moreover, although affection, for the most part, commonly precedes friendship yet it ought never be followed unless reason lead it, honor temper it, and justice rule it. 58. Hence, this friendship which we have styled puerile, because it is chiefly in children that feelings hold sway, ought, as a thing unfaithful, unstable, and always mixed with impure loves, to be guarded against in every way by those who take delight in the sweetness of spiritual friendship. We call it not friendship but friendship's poison since the proper bounds of love, which extend from soul to soul, can never be observed in it. Rather rising like a mist from the concupiscence of the flesh it obscures and corrupts the true character of friendship, and through neglect of the spirit it draws one to the desires of the flesh.[68] 59. For that reason the beginnings of spiritual friendship ought to possess, first of all, purity of intention, the direction of reason and the restraint of moderation; and thus the very desire for such friendship, so sweet as it comes upon us, will presently make friendship itself a delight to experience, so that it will never cease to be properly ordered.[69]

Then there is the friendship which is based on a likeness in evil. Of this type I refrain from speaking, since, as we have said before, it is not to be considered even worthy of the name of friendship.

60. There is, besides, a friendship which the consideration of some advantage excites and which many think ought to be sought, encouraged, and preserved for this reason.[70] But if we admit this type, how many most worthy of all love shall we exclude, those, namely, who, since they have nothing and possess nothing, offer, assuredly, no material gain or hope therefore to anyone! 61. But if you include among "advantages," counsel in doubt, consolation in adversity, and other benefits of like nature—these in any case, are to be expected from a friend, but they ought to follow friendship, not precede it. For he has not yet learned what friendship is who wishes any reward other than itself.[71] Such a reward friendship will certainly be for those cultivating it, when, wholly translated to God, it immerses in the divine contemplation those whom it has united. 62. For, although friendship, sure of its blessings, brings many great advantages, nevertheless we are certain that friendship does not proceed from the advantages but rather the advantages proceed from it.[72] Indeed, we do not believe that a friendship arose between those great men because of the benefits which Barzillai, the Gileadite, bestowed on David when he was fleeing from his parricide son, receiving him, taking care of him, counting him among his friends, but rather we do not doubt that such favor proceeded from friendship itself. For there is no one who thinks that the king was in need of that man previous to his friendship with him.[73] 63. Indeed, that he himself, a man of great wealth, hoped for no recompense from the king for his deeds one can clearly observe from the fact that when the king so generously offered him all the delights and riches of the state, he would not agree to take anything, preferring to be content with what he had.[74] Similarly, we know that the sacred bond of friendship between David and Jonathan, which was consecrated not through the hope of future advantage, but from the contemplation of virtue,[75] was very profitable for both. The life of the one was preserved by the ingenuity of the other but to his own benefit, in that his own posterity was thus preserved.[76] 64. Since, therefore, among the good, friendship always precedes and advantage follows, surely, it is not so much the benefit obtained through a friend that delights as the friend's love in itself.[77]

Now, then, whether we have said enough on the fruits of friendship or indicated clearly among which individuals it can begin, be preserved, and be perfected; whether, besides, we have plainly disclosed the flattering subserviency which is clothed with the false name of friendship, and whether also we have set forth the definite limits up to which love among friends ought to be extended: of all these questions you yourselves be the judges.

65. *Gratian.* I do not recall that this last point was sufficiently explained.

66. *Aelred.* But you remember, I think, that I refuted the opinion of those who establish the limits of friendship at agreement on vices and evil deeds; of those also, who think that one ought to go so far as to suffer exile and any form of dishonor, provided no harm is done to one's neighbor. 67. But I have also refuted the opinion of those who measure out their friendship with the yardstick of advantages anticipated. However, two of those forms of friendship which Walter proposed I did not consider even worthy of mention. For what can be more absurd than to extend friendship to the mere mutual repayment of one's friend through services and compliments, since all things ought to be in common among those who should indeed be of one mind and one soul?[78] How base this, too, would be, for anyone to regard his friend only in the same way he regards himself, since each ought to have a low opinion of himself and a high opinion of his friend!

68. Then, when we had completely disposed of these false ends of friendship, we thought that the true end ought to be set forth from the words of the Lord, who has taught that death itself in behalf of a friend should not be shunned. But in order that base individuals thus disposed and willing to die for one another might not be regarded as having reached the zenith of friendship, we further indicated among which persons friendship can arise and be perfected. Then we expressed the belief that those, who, on account of the many anxieties and cares which friendship entails, think it should for that reason be avoided, ought to be charged with absurdity. Finally, we explained as briefly as possible which friendships ought to be avoided by all good people.

69. It is clear, then, from this whole discussion, what the fixed and true limit of spiritual friendship is: namely, that nothing ought to be denied to a friend, nothing ought to be refused for a friend, which

is less than the very precious life of the body, which divine authority has taught should be laid down for a friend. Hence, since the life of the soul is of far greater excellence than that of the body, any action, we believe, should be altogether denied a friend which brings about the death of the soul, that is, sin, which separated God from the soul and the soul from life. But what limit ought to be preserved and what caution be maintained in those actions which one should perform for a friend, or tolerate in his behalf, this is not the time to decide.

70. *Gratian.* I admit that our friend Walter has benefited me not a little. In response to his questioning, you have summed up in a brief epilogue the principal points of the discussion, and have, so to speak, fixed them in the memory. And now, please tell us what limit should be preserved in serving one's friends, and what caution should be kept in mind.

71. *Aelred.* Both these and other matters pertaining to friendship remain to be discussed. But an hour has already passed, and these others who have just arrived are by their impatience, as you see, hustling me off to other business.

72. *Walter.* You may be sure I leave unwillingly. Tomorrow, indeed, when occasion presents itself, I intend to return. And let our friend Gratian see to it that he is on time tomorrow morning, that he may not accuse us of neglect, or we accuse him of tardiness.

Dwelling in Friendship

- What image of Aelred has developed by the close of Book Two? Walter's and Gratian's religious superior? Their wise and insightful teacher? A trusted friend? Perhaps a combination of all three? Why does Aelred have such long interventions in this section of the dialogue? Does he provide an adequate summary of the discussion? Why is Walter disappointed that they must postpone their conversation until the next day?

✣

Book Two Review

- Do you agree with Aelred that friendship is essential for happiness in this life? Do you agree with him that it is essential for happiness in the life to come? Why is it so important for human beings to have close bonds of friendship? What does it say about human nature? What does it say about what we yearn for? What does it tell us about our yearning for God? What does it say about God's yearning for us?

- Do you think that spiritual friendships are very common? Do you know any people who share such a deep friendship? Have you yourself ever experienced such a friendship? What role does God play in the formation of such friendships? What role do the individuals themselves play in forming them? How do such friends relate to each other? How do such friends relate to God?

- Do you agree with Aelred that only the good can become true friends? Do you think he went too far in making such a claim? Why is he so firm in this position? What does he mean by it? What does he not mean? Do you agree with his description of what it means to be a "good person?" Would you add anything to it? Would you take anything away? What are the strengths of his description? What are its weaknesses? How does the good person deal with his or her faults and imperfections?

- Do you like Aelred's metaphor of the threefold kiss? If so, what do you like about it? Is there anything you dislike about it? Do you think it is an appropriate metaphor for describing growth in the spiritual life today? Do you think that the corporeal, spiritual, and mystical levels exhaust the possible ways in which the metaphor of the kiss can be applied? Are there any dimensions of our human makeup that Aelred's metaphor overlooks?

- Does Aelred's presentation of puerile, advantageous, and spiritual friendships add anything to his earlier description in Book One of carnal, worldly, and spiritual friendships? What are the strengths and weaknesses of this most recent presentation? Which of the two presentations do you prefer? Do they conflict in any way? In what way do they complement each other? On a more personal level, do you believe it possible for two friends to move from one kind of friendship to another? Do you believe it possible for two friends to regress from an advanced form of friendship to an earlier form? Do you believe it possible for two friends to experience two or more of these friendships simultaneously? What has been your experience? What do you think Aelred would say?

Book Three

The Conditions
and Characters
Requisite for Unbroken
Friendship

⁜

Book Three: An Overview

In this third and final book, Aelred develops a number of themes about
the process involved in forming deep friendships and maintaining
them. For example, in a fallen world that so often seems full of darkness
and division, he sees friendship as a carefully tended garden in which
the seeds of reciprocated love are carefully watered, tended, and grown.
Because of our weakened and fragile condition, we must take care in
choosing our friends and test them in order to be sure of their worthiness. While Aelred offers a concrete list of the bad habits and behaviors
detrimental to forming lasting friendships, he does not mean to imply
that we can become friends only with those who are already perfect.

On the contrary, friendship, for him, is an instrument that helps people grow in holiness and travel along the road to perfection. In this life, all friendships are touched with imperfection; only in the next life will true and authentic friendships be entirely without stain. Until then, we must take care to nurture and even protect our friendships the best we know how. Aelred insists, however, that some habits of thought and action are so infectious and demeaning that a true friendship will have little if any hope of surviving their constant influence. Slander, reproach, pride, disclosing secrets, and secret detraction are so harmful to the formation of true friendship that it is better not to even try to befriend people who continuously display them.

When reading Aelred's presentation of the various stages of friendship, some may get the feeling that he is too calculating, perhaps even callous, in describing the way we should scrutinize candidates for both selection and admission to friendship. Such a judgment, however, would be overly harsh, since Aelred is simply being realistic. While he may seem a bit romantic when discussing the ideal of perfect friendship, he is very pragmatic when talking about actual friendships in the real world. He is a man of faith, yet someone whose feet are firmly planted on the ground. He knows from his own experience that friendships that are not carefully selected and tested will unravel in the midst of the internal and external pressures around them. He does not apologize for the demands he makes on those whom he would befriend. True friendship, in his mind, does not simply happen. It comes about, in part, through God's graceful movement in the hearts of those whom he calls and, in part, through those who strive to cooperate with that grace by doing their utmost to enter into friendships based on the love of God and neighbor.

When selecting friends, Aelred wants us not only to avoid troublesome characters, but also to actively seek out people with positive attributes. A true friend, in his mind, should be loyal, well intentioned, discrete, and patient. Each of these qualities should be tested in matters both large and small. These qualities are important because friends should feel free to share with one another their deepest, most intimate concerns. They rest in each other's hearts and reveal to each other their triumphs and joys, as well as their problems and difficulties. Friends walk in each other's light and darkness. They must know how to give and receive, how to listen and discern, how to support yet also challenge. We should admit a person into the bond of friendship only after he or she has demonstrated over time the capacity to relate in this way. We befriend one another so that we may find ourselves in the other person—and vice versa. Aelred believes that such friendships can and will come about only if those involved in them are rooted in God and reciprocate their love for one another by actively seeking each other's well-being. Because of the close, intimate nature of this bond, we should not enter into it or withdraw from it without serious forethought and reflection.

Aelred gives sound advice not only on how we should enter into friendship, but also on how we should end it. He is adamant that true friendship is eternal, but understands that sometimes people mistake a much weaker bond for a profound spiritual tie. For this reason, he draws an important distinction between true and apparent friendship, between a bond of intimate companionship that is true and lasting and one that is ephemeral and short-lived. He counsels prudence to those of us who find ourselves in a situation where what we thought was a sound spiritual friendship was found to be otherwise. Rather than ending the relationship abruptly, he advises us to unravel the friendship "stitch-by-stitch" over an extended period of time. In doing so, there will be no hard feelings between those involved and, while no longer friends, they will be able to relate to one another with dignity and mutual respect. Aelred reminds us, moreover, that even though we will no longer share sentiments of affection, security, and happiness with a person we once called a friend, we are still bound to relate to him or her at all times in a loving manner.

In addition to giving concrete criteria about the qualities that candidates for friendship should and should not have, as well as how we should go about testing them, Aelred also responds to the question about the wisdom of having friends in the first place. To many, the potential risk of failure and the heartbreak that will almost surely follow are reasons enough for avoiding any close personal ties. Such a risk is compounded by an overly individualistic understanding of human nature that emphasizes personal achievement and self-reliance to the exclusion of intimate relationships. Aelred could not disagree more with such people. He asserts the social nature of human existence, a belief surely supported by the communal style of living espoused by the monastic ideal that he lived and to which he was so dedicated. In his mind, the need for companionship is so deeply rooted in our hearts that it would be impossible for us to enjoy anything without it. Our yearning for friendship says something about the very fabric of our lives and about the nature of God in whose image, as Aelred so firmly believed, we are made. Happiness, he believes, is rooted in our desire to share with others. A human heart bereft of friendship is sterile and empty. Nothing will satisfy it but the embrace of human companionship. A person without friends is doomed to a life of sadness and desperation; a person with friends, by way of contrast, has found the heart's greatest treasure and the key to a happy life.

Aelred speaks from experience and cites many examples from his own life. He tells us about how he treated a friend with a hot temper, about how he himself went about choosing some of his closest friends, and about how he dealt with the bestowal of offices on these friends. He goes to great pains not to leave his discussion of spiritual friendship on a merely theoretical level, but to root it concretely in his own personal experience. This emphasis on experience is an important aspect of the monastic (as opposed to scholastic) approach to theology and is evidenced not just in Book Three, but throughout the whole treatise. The success of the work depends not on its ideas or literary style, but on whether it has helped us to experience this elusive goal for ourselves.

In addition to including his own personal experience, Aelred makes good use of the three other major sources that he uses in his treatise: Cicero's *On Friendship,* the Church fathers, and sacred scripture. His many allusions and direct quotations from Cicero's treatise demonstrate his belief that even pagan and secular learning, limited and incomplete though it may be, can offer important insights into human nature. He can hold such a position, however, only because he believes that human nature was not totally corrupted as a result of humanity's fall from grace and that careful reflection on human existence can provide sound insights into what it means to be human. He is also well aware that human learning, however sophisticated, can only go so far, and that it needs to be supplemented by the insights of Christian revelation, especially the scriptures and the insights of the Church fathers. St. Jerome's statement that true friendship is eternal provides one of the underlying presuppositions of the entire treatise and is one of the focal points for Aelred's presentation of the necessary conditions and prerequisites for unbroken friendship. He also makes good use of St. Ambrose's Duties of the Clergy to emphasize the equality and intimate nature of the sharing between true friends. Aelred's use of Cicero and the Church fathers in Book Three, however, pales in comparison to his use of scripture. Quotations from both the Old Testament and the New Testament appear on nearly every page of Book Three. Aelred uses these scriptural examples to further develop his insights into true spiritual friendship, and to set his teaching on a firm Christian foundation. By the time we get to the end of the treatise, there can be little doubt in anyone's mind that spiritual friendship comes from God and has the authority of God's Word behind it. Aelred's deep regard for the authority of sacred scripture and his successful attempt to root his teaching on friendship in its pages reflect his desire to have all of life permeated and taken over by the transforming power of God's Word.

Finally, it bears noting that Aelred fills Book Three with many practical distinctions intended to assist his readers in making appropriate decisions about whom they should befriend, how these candidates should be tested, when they should be admitted, and how they should be enjoyed. At first sight, we might be led to think that distinctions related to the difference between love and friendship, virtue and vice, true and apparent friendship, simulation and dissimulation have more to do with scholastic method than with a monastic treatise on friendship. We should not forget, however, that the scholastic method's love of rational distinctions arose, at least in part, out of the monastic love of learning, and that the monastic virtue of discretion, the ability to make wise and prudent decisions, requires a capacity to distinguish good from evil in the circumstances of everyday life. The practical nature of Book Three reflects Aelred's sincere desire that we make good decisions when choosing our friends and fostering close spiritual ties. In the final analysis, the positive and negative qualities of a potential friend, the various stages of friendship, the testing required, even the description of the process of how we should cultivate friendship until it reaches its perfection in the next life are all about making good distinctions and sound judgments in life. Here, the practical scope of Aelred's monastic background comes to the fore and leads us to a simple yet undeniable truth. We carefully select and scrutinize so many things in our daily lives, from the clothes we wear, to the food we eat, to the means by which we travel. Should we not be at least equally selective and judicious about the friends we make? Aelred believes we should. His treatise bears the mark of truth and has much relevance for our lives today.

Book Three: 1–13

Introduction

In Book Three, Aelred, Walter, and Gratian meet again during their free time and resume their discussion from the previous day. This time, they focus on such issues as the extent to which one should go in serving one's friends and the caution one should have when selecting them. The discussion begins with the good-natured humor that the reader has come to expect from Walter and Gratian. It is clear from the outset that they wish to make good use of the time available to them (no. 1).

As they get into their topic, Aelred makes an astute observation about the relationship between love and friendship. Love can exist without friendship, he says, but not vice versa (no. 2). Walter asks if everyone we love should be admitted to friendship (no. 4). Aelred responds that love of God is the very foundation of spiritual friendship (no. 5), but not everyone we love should be admitted to friendship (no. 6). Those who are going to be the intimate companions of our souls must be carefully selected and tried before being admitted to friendship (no. 6). He outlines four stages by which two persons enter the heights of spiritual friendship: selection, probation, admission, and perfect harmony in matters human and divine with charity and benevolence (no. 8). When asked by Walter if this definition of friendship as perfect harmony applies to all of the various types of friendship described earlier in the treatise, Aelred insists that it applies only to true friendship (no. 10). When asked by Gratian why the definition of friendship as a community of likes and dislikes is not correct, Aelred responds that it is acceptable for those whose lives are well ordered and under control (no. 12).

Text

1. *Aelred.* Where have you come from and why have you come?

Gratian. Surely you know why I am here.

Aelred. Isn't Walter present?

Gratian. Let him see to that himself; surely he cannot accuse us of tardiness today.

Aelred. Do you want to follow up the questions which have been proposed?

Gratian. I have confidence in Walter, for I confess I do need his presence. He is quicker in grasping things, better at questioning, and has a better memory, also.

(Enter Walter)

Aelred. Did you hear that, Walter? Gratian is more friendly to you than you thought.

Walter. How could he fail to be my friend, since he is everybody's friend? But now that we are both here, mindful of your promise, let us show that we appreciate this free time.

2. *Aelred.* The fountain and source of friendship is love. There can be love without friendship, but friendship without love is impossible. Love proceeds either from nature, or from duty, from reason alone, or from affection alone, and sometimes from both simultaneously—from nature, as a mother loves her child; from duty, when through giving and receiving, some men are joined by special affection; from reason alone, as we love our enemies, not as the result of a spontaneous inclination of the heart but from the necessity of precept; from affection alone, when anyone, because of bodily qualities only, such as beauty, strength, eloquence, inclines the affection of others to himself. 3. From reason and affection simultaneously, when he, whom reason urges should be loved because of the excellence of his virtue, steals into the soul of another by the mildness of his character and the charm of a praise-worthy life. In this way reason unites with affection so that the love is pure because of reason and sweet because of affection. Which of these types of love seems to you more advantageous to friendship?[1]

4. *Walter.* Indeed, the last, which contemplation of virtue forms and charm of character adorns. But I wish to know whether all whom we love in this manner should be admitted to that sweet mystery of friendship?

5. *Aelred.* In the first place, one ought to lay a solid foundation for spiritual love itself, and in this foundation its principles ought to be set down, so that those who are mounting straight up to its higher levels may not neglect or go beyond its foundation, but observe the greatest caution. That foundation is the love of God,[2] to which all things that either love or affection suggests, all that secretly any spirit or openly any friend recommends, must be referred. Moreover, one ought to observe carefully that whatever is built thereon conforms to the foundation. Have no doubt that whatever is seen as going beyond this foundation ought to be brought back into conformity with its plan and set right according to its nature.

6. And yet, not all whom we love should be received into friendship, for not all are found worthy of it. For since your friend is the companion of your soul, to whose spirit you join and attach yours, and so associate yourself that you wish to become one instead of two, since he is one to whom you entrust yourself as to another self, from whom you hide nothing, from whom you fear nothing,[3] you should, in the first place, surely choose one who is considered fitted for all this. Then he is to be tried, and so finally admitted. For friendship should be stable and manifest a certain likeness to eternity, persevering always in affection.[4] 7. And so we ought not, like children, change friends by reason of some vagrant whim.[5] For since there is no one more detestable than the man who injures friendship, and nothing torments the mind more than desertion or insult at the hands of a friend, a friend ought to be chosen with the utmost care and tested with extreme caution. But once admitted, he should be so borne with, so treated, so deferred to, that, as long as he does not withdraw irrevocably from the established foundation, he is yours, and you are his, in body as well as in spirit, so that there will be no division of minds, affections, wills, or judgments.[6] 8. You see, therefore, the four stages by which one climbs to the perfection of friendship: the first is selection, the second probation, the third admission, and the fourth perfect harmony in matters human and divine with charity and benevolence.[7]

9. *Walter.* I recall that you proved this definition satisfactorily in that first discussion of yours with your well loved Ivo; but since you treated of many types of friendship, I should like to know whether this definition includes them all.

10. *Aelred.* No; for since true friendship can exist only among the good[8] who can exhibit neither wish nor action detrimental to faith or

good morals, this definition naturally does not embrace every friend-ship but only that friendship which is true.

11. *Gratian.* Why should not that definition which pleased me so much before yesterday's discussion be equally approved, namely, the one which defines friendship as a community of likes and dislikes?[9]

12. *Aelred.* Certainly. Among those whose habits have been cor-rected, whose life is well ordered and whose affections are controlled, I think your definition need not be rejected.

13. *Walter.* Let Gratian see to it that these conditions be found not only in himself but also in the one he loves so that he will have the same likes and dislikes as his friend. Wishing nothing for himself, let him neither grant anything that is unjust, dishonorable, or unbecom-ing. But we are waiting to learn from you more about those four stages which you mentioned above.

Dwelling in Friendship

- Is there any significance to Aelred's beginning each of his three books with a different dialogue partner: Ivo in Book One, Walter in Book Two, and now Gratian in Book Three? Is there any significance to his moving the conversation from two persons to three much more quickly in Book Three than in Book Two? Does he pretty much pick up his conversation with Walter and Gratian where he left it the day before? Is the transition from Book Two to Book Three smoother than that from Book One to Book Two?

Book Three: 14–38

✤

Introduction

Responding to Walter's request, Aelred begins to explain the four stages necessary for entering into spiritual friendship. With regard to selection, the first stage, he says that we should enter into friendship only with those who lead virtuous lives and not those with evil habits (no. 14). We should not consider those who are inconstant, mistrustful, talkative, and prone to anger as viable candidates for friendship (no. 14). When both Walter and Gratian question him about his own friendship with someone with an irascible bent (nos. 16, 18), Aelred responds that once such people are accepted into friendship, they should be loved and dealt with patiently as long as there is no question of acting inappropriately (nos. 17, 20).

In response to Walter, he then outlines the five vices that would disqualify a person as a candidate for spiritual friendship. Even when it is not believed and done out of anger, slander ruins a person's reputation and is a sign of broken confidence (no. 23). Even when false, reproach embarrasses and makes the innocent man blush (no. 24). For its lack of humility and inability to admit guilt, pride prevents a broken friendship from being healed (no. 24). Disclosing of secrets fills all concerned with resentment, hatred, and grief (no. 24). Secret detraction attacks from behind and betrays the trust upon which friendship is based. We should avoid anyone who exhibits any of these vices and should not choose him for a friend until he repents (no. 26). He then offers numerous examples from scripture to support his claims (nos. 26–28). In addition to these vices, Aelred also claims that those prone to excessive anger, the fickle, and the suspicious should also be avoided when selecting friends (nos. 28–30). Walter wonders if it is possible to find a person who does not display any of the above vices (no. 31). Although it is not easy to find someone who never succumbs to such actions, Aelred insists that there are many who act virtuously and have learned to control these disordered passions. Such people should be preferred, since they are better prepared for the demands of spiritual friendship (no. 32).

When pushed by Gratian, Aelred admits that the friend of whom he was speaking earlier is, in fact, prone to acting out of an irascible nature, but that this side of him does not surface within the bounds of their friendship (nos. 33–36). Furthermore, Aelred claims, friendship has affected an overall change for the good in the irascible monk. Denying the contention that he is simply being patient with his friend (Aelred points out that such "patience" oftentimes only brings out the worst in those who suffer with anger), Aelred claims that due to the cultivation of true friendship, he is able to help his friend sincerely temper his anger. In Aelred's presence, the monk is far less likely to lash out. Instead, he stays calm in challenging situations and discusses them later with Aelred in private. This is obviously a change for the good, such that Aelred claims that he can make his friend's anger subside with a mere nod of his head, even when it is on the verge of erupting (nos. 37–38).

✢

Text

1 4. *Aelred.* First of all, then, let us deal with selection itself. Now there are certain vices such that, if anyone has been involved in them, he will not long preserve the laws or rights of friendship. Persons of this type should not readily be chosen for friendship; but if their life and habits be found pleasing in other respects, one should deal energetically with them, to the end that they may be healed and so considered fitted for friendship. Such persons are, for example, the irascible, the fickle, the suspicious, and the garrulous. 15. Indeed, it is difficult for one subject to the frenzy of anger not to rise up sometime against his friend, as it is written in Ecclesiasticus: "There is a friend that will disclose hatred and strife and reproaches."[10] Therefore Scripture says: "Be not a friend to an angry man, and do not walk with a furious man, lest he become a snare for your soul."[11] And Solomon: "Anger rests in the bosom of a fool."[12] And who does not think it impossible to preserve friendship for long with a fool?

16. *Walter.* But we have seen you, if we are not mistaken, with deep devotion cultivate a friendship with a very irascible man, and we have

heard, he was never hurt by you even to the end of his life, though he often offended you.

17. *Aelred.* There are some individuals who have a natural bent toward anger, yet who are accustomed so to restrain and overcome this passion that they never give way to those five vices which Scripture testifies dissolve and break friendship.[13] However, they may occasionally offend a friend by a thoughtless word or act or by a zeal that fails in discretion. If it happens that we have received such men into our friendship, we must bear with them patiently. And since their affection toward us is established with certainty, if then there is any excess in word or action, this ought to be put up with as being in a friend, or at least our admonition of his fault ought to be administered painlessly and even pleasantly.

18. *Gratian.* A few days ago that friend of yours, whom many think you prefer to all of us, was, so we thought, overcome by anger, and said and did something that everyone could see displeased you. Yet we do not believe or see that he has in any degree lost favor with you. Hence we are not a little surprised that, when we speak together, you will not neglect anything that pleases him no matter how trivial it may be, yet he cannot bear even trifles for your sake.

19. *Walter.* Gratian is far bolder than I am; for I was aware of these facts, but knowing your feeling toward him, I did not dare to say anything to you about the matter.

20. *Aelred.* Certainly that man is very dear to me. Having once received him into my friendship, I can never do otherwise than love him. Therefore, if perhaps I was stronger than he was in this instance, and since the wills of both did not fuse into one, it was easier for me to yield my will than he his. And since there was no question of any dishonor being involved, and as confidence was not violated, or virtue lessened, it was right for me to yield to my friend that I might bear with him when he seemed to have transgressed, and that, when his peace was endangered, I might prefer his will to mine.

21. *Walter.* But since your former friend has passed away, and this other has satisfied you, although we do not see how, I would like to have you explain to us those five vices by which friendship is so injured as to be dissolved, in order that we may be able to avoid those who ought in no wise be chosen as friends.

22. *Aelred.* Listen, then, not to my words, but to Scripture: "He that upbraids his friend, breaks friendship. Although he has drawn a

sword at a friend, despair not; for there may be a returning to a friend. If he opens a sad mouth, fear not."[14] Consider what this means. If your friend, overcome by anger, chances to draw a sword or utter a grievous word, if, as though not loving you, he for a time withdraws himself from you, if sometimes he prefers his own counsel to yours, if he disagrees with you in any opinion or discussion, do not think your friendship must be dissolved because of these differences. 23. "For," says Scripture, "there may be a reconciliation with your friend except in the case of upbraiding, reproach, pride, disclosing of secrets or a treacherous wound; for in all these cases a friend will flee away."[15]

Let us then more carefully consider these five vices, that we may not bind ourselves by the ties of friendship to persons whom either the fury of anger or some other passion is wont to incite to these vices. Slander, indeed, injures reputation and extinguishes love, for such is the wickedness of men, that whenever a friend makes a charge against a friend under the impulse of anger, even though it is not believed, it is yet broadcast as if it were the utterance of a confidant of secrets. 24. For just as many are delighted at praise of themselves, so too do they find joy in reproaches against their neighbors. What is more impious than reproach which suffuses the countenance of an innocent man with a pitiable blush even when the charge is false? But what is less to be endured than pride, which excludes the remedy of humility and admission of guilt by which alone the broken friendship could have been healed? It renders a man bold in wrongdoing and passionate in recrimination. Then follows the revelation of hidden things, that is, of secrets, than which nothing is more base, nothing more detestable, leaving no love and no charm between friends, but filling all with the bitterness of indignation and sprinkling all with the venom of hatred and grief. 25. Hence it is written: "He that discloses the secret of a friend loses his credit."[16] And a little later: "To disclose the secrets of a friend leaves no hope to an unhappy soul."[17] For what is more unfortunate than the man who loses faith and languishes in despair. The last vice by which friendship is dissolved is treacherous persecution, which is nothing other than secret detraction. A treacherous blow indeed, it is the death-dealing blow of the serpent and the asp. "If a serpent bite in silence," says Solomon, "he is no better who backbites secretly."[18] 26. Therefore, should you discover anyone habituated to these vices, you ought to avoid him, nor, until he repents, should he be chosen for friendship. Let us renounce slander, the avenger of which is

God. Shimei, attacking holy David with insults as he was fleeing from
the face of Absalom, was, according to the testamentary words which
the dying father bequeathed to his son, decreed by the authority of the
Holy Spirit to be worthy of death.[19] Let us then shun recriminations.
The unhappy Nabel of Carmel, reproaching David with his servitude
and his flight, merited to be cut down by the Lord and killed.[20] But if
we chance to have failed in the law of friendship toward anyone, let
us shun pride and seek to win back the favor of our friend by some
humble service. 27. When King David mercifully offered friendship
to Hanun, the son of Nabash, a friendship such as he had formerly
displayed to Nabash, the king of the children of Ammon, Hanun,
arrogant and ungrateful to his friend, added contumely to contempt.[21]
For this reason fire and sword together consumed him as well as his
people and his cities. But above all things, let us consider it a sacrilege
to reveal the secrets of friends, an act by which confidence is lost and
despair is borne in upon the captive soul. Hence it is that the impious
Ahithophel, casting his lot with the parricide Absalom, after he had
betrayed to him David's plan, presently saw that the plan he himself
had proposed in opposition was not being put into effect; thereupon
he took his own life by hanging—an end worthy of a traitor.[22] 28.
Finally, let us consider it the poison of friendship to slander a friend,
an act which caused the face of Mary to be covered with leprosy, and
caused her to be cast outside the camp for six days, and to be deprived
of association with the people.[23]

Not only men of excessive anger but also the fickle and the suspicious should be avoided in this selection of friends.[24] For since a great
fruit of friendship is the security whereby you entrust and commit
yourself to a friend, how can there be any security in the love of him
who is tossed about by every wind, who consents to every counsel?
The disposition of such a man, like soft clay, receives and fashions
diverse and opposing images the livelong day, at the whim of him
who wishes to impress them. 29. Besides, what is more in accord with
friendship than a certain mutual peace and tranquility of heart, which
the suspicious man never knows, since he is never at rest?[25] In truth the
suspicious man is ever ridden by his curiosity, which pricks him with
relentless spurs and has an inexhaustible supply of fuel for the fires of
uneasiness and anxiety that burn under him. For if he sees his friend
speaking secretly with anyone, he thinks he is betrayed. If his friend
shows himself kind to another, or pleasant, he cries out that he himself

is loved the less. If his friend rebukes him, he interprets this as hatred. If his friend believes him worthy of praise, he charges falsely that he is being mocked. 30. Neither do I think the one who is garrulous should be chosen, because a talkative man will not be justified.[26] "Do you see," says the Wise Man, "a person over-ready with his tongue? There is more hope for a fool than for such a one."[27] That man, therefore, should be chosen as your friend whom the fury of anger does not disturb, nor instability divide, nor suspicion consume, nor garrulity sunder from the gravity which ought to be his. It is particularly advantageous for you to choose one who conforms to your habits, who harmonizes with your disposition. "Indeed, among dissimilar characters," as blessed Ambrose remarks, "friendship cannot exist; therefore, the grace of each ought to be mutually consonant."[28]

31. *Walter.* But where can such a man be found, one who is neither irascible, nor unstable, nor suspicious? For as to the over-talkative man, he cannot escape notice.

32. *Aelred.* Although it is not easy to find one who is never moved by these passions, there surely are many who are found to be superior to all of them; men who suppress anger with patience, restrain levity by preserving gravity, drive out suspicions by the contemplation of love. I should say that such men ought to be chosen by preference for friendship on the ground that they are better trained in it. Because they conquer vice with virtue, their friendship is the more enduring as their resistance to temptation is the more valiant.

33. *Gratian.* Please, do not be angry if I speak. With respect to that friend of yours, of whom we made mention a little while ago, and whom, we do not doubt, you have received into your friendship, I should like to know whether he seems irascible to you.

34. *Aelred.* He is, indeed; but in friendship, hardly at all.

35. *Gratian.* What do you mean, not to be angry in friendship?

36. *Aelred.* You do not doubt that friendship exists between us?

Gratian. Not at all.

Aelred. When have you heard of anger, strife, dissensions, rivalries, or disputes arising between us?

Gratian. Never, but we attribute this not to his, but to your patience.

37. *Aelred.* You are mistaken. For anger which is not held in check by affection can in no wise be checked by the patience of some other person. On the contrary, patience excites the irascible man to fury[29] and

he hopes to get a crumb of comfort from the possibility that another may show himself to be his match in vituperation. Indeed, he about whom we are now speaking, preserves the law of friendship toward me in such a way that I can restrain an outburst at any time by a mere nod, even when it is already breaking forth into speech, so that he never reveals in public what is displeasing but always waits till we are alone to unburden his mind's thought. 38. Now, if, instead of friendship, nature prescribed this course of action to him, I would judge him neither so virtuous nor so worthy of praise. If, indeed, as is sometimes the case, my feeling differs from his, we give in to each other so that sometimes he yields to me, but generally I yield to him.

Dwelling in Friendship

- What is your initial reaction to Aelred's emphasis on the careful selection of friends? Does it make sense to you? Do you have a difficult time accepting the idea? Do you agree with his list of the vices that would disqualify a candidate for friendship? Are there any you would add or cross off from his list? Do you select your friends with care? Do you think you should?

Book Three: 39–59

⁘

Introduction

Walter wonders what one should do if one enters into friendship with someone who already has one or more of these vices or develops them at a later time (no. 39). In response, Aelred says that special care should be taken to avoid such friends in the selection process and during their probation period (no. 40). If such an ill-fated friendship should develop, however, it should not be broken off immediately, but "unstitched little by little" and in such a way so as not to arouse animosity (nos. 41–42). If ill feelings do arise and enmity ensues, Aelred says one should accord honor to the old friendship by enduring as much as possible whatever insults follow (nos. 43–44). Aelred reminds Walter and Gratian that friendship is eternal and that one is bound to love at all times. Should a friend act in such a way that friendship must be withdrawn, we are still bound to love him (no. 44).

When Walter asks what faults would require gradually dissolving a friendship, Aelred says the five faults listed earlier would qualify, as well as a sixth: if your friend harms someone you are bound to love and if he persists in such behavior even after being brought to task for it (no. 46). He cites numerous examples from scripture to support his claims (no. 47). Quoting St. Jerome, he reminds Walter and Gratian that a true friendship never ends and that even after a friendship is dissolved, a friend should still love, honor, bless, and do good for the one who now scorns him (no. 49). Walter wonders if with such actions toward another, one can really say that the friendship has been dissolved (no. 50). Aelred responds by saying that friendship contains four elements: love, affection, security, and happiness (no. 51). Although some traces may remain, affection, security, and happiness are normally lost when a friendship is dissolved. Love, however, must never be withdrawn (no. 52). At this point, Aelred expresses a desire to move on with the discussion (no. 53). Walter, however, asks for a brief summary of what they have covered in their conversation and Aelred concurs (nos. 54-59).

✧

Text

39. *Walter.* Gratian has had sufficient attention. Now I should like to have you explain this to me: suppose one should somewhat heedlessly chance to contact friendship with characters such as those whom you said a little while ago we should avoid, or suppose those who you said should be chosen should fall into these vices or perhaps even into worse ones, what sort of loyalty ought then to be preserved toward them and what sort of favor ought to be shown them?

40. *Aelred.* Obviously these things should, if possible, be guarded against in the act of choosing friends and also during their probation, so that, indeed, we may not form intimacies too quickly, particularly with those unworthy of such regard. Now, they are worthy of friendship in whose very selves there is reason why they should be loved.[30] And yet, even in those who are thought to have been tried and found worthy, faults often betray themselves, at one time to the injury of their friends, at another to that of strangers; and in the latter case, the disgrace of their action falls back upon their friends.[31] With such friends all care must be taken that they may be made to amend their lives. 41. But if this is impossible, I think friendship should not be broken off or dissolved, but, as someone has well said, "it should rather be unstitched little by little,[32] unless perchance some insufferable offense flames out to full view, so that it is neither right nor honorable not to effect an immediate estrangement or separation."[33] For if a friend undertakes anything either against his father or against his country which demands sudden and hurried correction, the demands of friendship will not be violated, if he is proclaimed a public and private enemy. 42. There are other faults for which, we think, friendship should not be broken off, as we have said, but dissolved gradually, yet in such a way that they do not result in enmities, from which spring quarrels, imprecations, and slanders.[34] For it is most shameful to wage a war of this kind with a man with whom you have lived on

terms of intimacy.[35] 43. For even if in all these ways you are assailed by him whom you had taken into your friendship (for with some men it is the way that, when they have so lived that they no longer deserve to be loved, if by chance some misfortune befalls them, they put the blame on their friend. They say that he has sinned against the laws of friendship, and every counsel which their friend gave they hold suspect. When they are unmasked and their fault is made public, not having anything else to do, they heap hatred and insults upon their friend, slandering him in corners, whispering in the dark, and telling lies to excuse themselves and accuse others[36]); 44. if, therefore, I say, you are attacked in all such ways after friendship has been severed, as long as the abuses are tolerable, they ought to be endured. This honor should be accorded to old friendship, that the fault should be in him who commits, but not to him who suffers, the wrong.[37] Friendship, indeed, is eternal; hence: "He that is a friend loves at all times."[38] If the one whom you love offends you, continue to love him despite the hurt. His conduct may compel the withdrawal of friendship, but never of love. Be concerned as much as you can for his welfare, safeguard his reputation, and never betray the secrets of his friendship, even though he should betray yours.

45. *Walter.* What are these faults, pray, for which you say friendship should be dissolved little by little?

46. *Aelred.* Those five which we described a little while ago, but especially the revelation of secrets and the hidden stings of detraction. To these five we add a sixth, namely, if your friend has injured those whom you are bound to love equally well, and if, even after he has been called to task, he continued to be an occasion of ruin and scandal to those for whose well-being you are responsible, especially when the infamy of these crimes is damaging to your own good name. For love ought not to outweigh religion, or faith, or charity toward one's neighbor, or the welfare of the people. 47. King Ahasuerus suspended on a cross the most haughty Aman, whom he had cherished above all others as his friend, preferring the welfare of his people and the love of his wife to the friendship which Aman had wounded by deceitful counsels.[39] And Jael, the wife of Heber the Klenite, although there was peace between Sisera and the house of Heber, nevertheless, preferring the welfare of her people to this friendship, put Sisera himself to sleep with a nail and hammer.[40] The holy prophet David according to the law of friendship ought to have spared the relations of

Jonathan. Nevertheless, hearing from the Lord that the people had suffered continually from hunger during three years "on account of Saul and his bloody house because he had killed the Gibeonites," he gave seven of Saul's relations to the Gibeonites to be punished.[41] 48. But I would not have you overlook this point, that between perfect friends, between friends who have been wisely chosen and prudently tested and are united by a genuinely spiritual friendship, no disagreements can possibly arise. For when friendship has made of two one, just as that which is one cannot be divided, so also friendship cannot be separated from itself. Therefore it is evident that a friendship, which permits of division, was never, in the respect in which it is injured, a true friendship at all, because "friendship which can end, was never true friendship."[42] 49. On the other hand, a friendship is the more laudable, and gives the greater proof of being a virtue, in proportion as the friend who has been wronged preserves it undiminished, loving him by whom he is no longer loved, honoring him by whom he is scorned, blessing him by whom he is cursed, and doing good to him who plots evil against him.

50. *Walter.* Now, therefore, can friendship be said to be dissolved, if such dispositions are to be manifested to the former friend by him who "dissolves" friendship?

51. *Aelred.* Four elements in particular seem to pertain to friendship: namely, love and affection, security and happiness. Love implies the rendering of services with benevolence, affection, an inward pleasure that manifests itself exteriorly; security, a revelation of all counsels and confidences without fear and suspicion; happiness, a pleasing and friendly sharing of all events which occur, whether joyful or sad, of all thoughts, whether harmful or useful, of everything taught or learned.[43] 52. Do you see in what respects friendship should be withdrawn from those who deserve to lose it? Surely that interior delight is withdrawn which drank continually from the heart of the friend; security is lost, by which it revealed its secrets to a friend; happiness is put aside, which friendly conversation produced. Therefore, that familiarity, in which such things find their place, must be denied a former friend, but love should not be withdrawn; yet all this should be done with a certain moderation and reverence, so that, if there has not been too great a shock, some traces of the former friendship always seem to remain.

53. *Gratian.* I certainly agree with what you say.

Aelred. Now turn your attention to selection, if I have said enough on these present points.

Walter. I should like a summary of the matter discussed to be given us in a brief recapitulation.

54. *Aelred.* I shall do as you wish. We have said that love is the source of friendship, not love of any sort whatever, but that which proceeds from reason and affection simultaneously, which, indeed, is pure because of reason and sweet because of affection. Then we said that a foundation of friendship should be laid in the love of God, to which all things which are proposed should be referred, and these ought to be examined as to whether they conform to the foundation or are at variance with it. 55. Then we thought that one should pay attention to the four steps which lead up to the heights of perfect friendship; for a friend ought first to be selected, next tested, then finally admitted, and from then on treated as a friend deserves. And speaking of selection, we excluded the quarrelsome, the irascible, the fickle, the suspicious, and the loquacious; and yet not all, but only those who are unable or unwilling to regulate or restrain these passions. For many are affected by these disturbances in such a manner that their perfection is not only in no way injured, but their virtue is even more laudably increased by the restraint of these passions. 56. For men, who, as though unbridled, are carried away headlong under the impulse of these passions, inevitably slip and fall into those vices by which friendship, as Scripture testifies, is wounded and dissolved; namely, insults, reproaches, betrayal of secrets, pride, and the stroke of treachery.[44] 57. If, nevertheless, you suffer all these evils from him whom you once received into friendship, we said that your friendship should not be broken off immediately, but dissolved little by little, and that such reverence should be maintained for the former friendship, that, although you withdraw your confidence from him, yet you never withdraw your love, refuse your aid, or deny him your advice. But if his frenzy breaks out even to blasphemies and calumny, do you, nevertheless, yield to the bonds of friendship, yield to charity, so that the blame will reside with him who inflicts, not with him who bears, the injury. 58. Furthermore, if he is found to be a peril to his father, to his country, to his fellow-citizens, to his dependents or to his friends, the bond of familiarity ought to be broken immediately; love for one man should not take precedence over the ruin of many. To prevent such

misfortunes one should be cautious in choosing a friend, that one be chosen whom fury does not goad on to such evils, nor levity induce, nor loquacity drive headlong, nor suspicion carry off; especially should one be chosen who does not differ too much from your character, and is not of harmony with your temperament. 59. But since we are speaking of true friendship, which cannot exist except among the good, we make no mention of those concerning whom there can be no doubt that they ought not to be chosen, namely, those who are base, avaricious, ambitious, slanderous. Now, then, if we have discussed selection sufficiently for you, let us then pass on to probation.

Walter. This is truly opportune, for I have my eye glued on the door for fear that someone may break in who will either put an end to our delights, or mingle some bitterness there-with, or introduce something trivial.

Dwelling in Friendship

- Does Aelred offer sound advice when he recommends ending a friendship gone awry "little by little"? Is this the only way of dealing appropriately with such a friendship? How do we tell when a friendship is beyond salvaging and when the two friends are simply encountering an obstacle to be faced squarely and overcome? Is Aelred's list of vices of any help? Is it difficult to continue loving someone who is no longer your friend?

Book Three: 60–75

✥

Introduction

Walter and Gratian are so interested in the discussion that they are guarding the door lest their conversation be interrupted (nos. 59–60). The brief pause gives Aelred the opportunity to move from the first to the second stage of spiritual direction, that is, from selection to probation (no. 61). He says that we must test four qualities in a friend—loyalty, right intention, discretion, and patience—and offers a brief description of each (no. 61). Loyalty is so important in friendship, he says, because friends must stick by one another in both good times and bad (no. 62). A friend must be tested in both small and great matters (no. 66). If a friend is found to be faithful even when others disparage our reputation, then we should not question his loyalty (no. 66). At this point Gratian reminds his abbot of one of his loyal friends from across the sea who was tested in this way, and then bids him to continue with his exposition (no. 67).

When discussing right intention, Aelred quotes the Gospel of Matthew for the formula of true friendship: "You shall love your neighbor as yourself" (Mt 22:39). A friend should love gratuitously, without any hope of reward (no. 69). He should not be interested in what he can gain from the friendship with regards to honor, glory, riches, or even freedom (no. 71). With regard to discretion, he states that we should test our friend for prudence and capacity to judge. Otherwise, our days will be spent in disagreement and endless quarrels (no. 72). Finally, we must test for patience, since without it we will not be able to put up with our friend in times of difficulty, especially when minor lapses and imperfections of character are revealed (nos. 73–74). Aelred concludes this section with an analogy from the marketplace. Just as many businessmen are experts in examining and selecting oxen, donkeys, sheep, and goats for their physical productivity, so should we devote ourselves to examining and testing those whom we wish to befriend. In his mind, it is madness not to do so (no. 75).

✣

Text

60. *Gratian.* The cellarer is coming; if you grant him admittance, you will have no opportunity of proceeding further. But see, I am guarding the door; do, Father, go on as you have begun.

61. *Aelred.* There are four qualities which must be tested in a friend: loyalty, right intention, discretion, and patience, that you may entrust yourself to him securely. The right intention, that he may expect nothing from your friendship except God and its natural good. Discretion, that he may understand what is to be done in behalf of a friend, what is to be sought from a friend, what sufferings are to be endured for his sake, upon what good deeds he is to be congratulated; and, since we think that a friend should sometimes be corrected, he must know for what faults this should be done, as well as the manner, the time, and the place. Finally, patience, that he may not grieve when rebuked, or despise or hate the one inflicting the rebuke, and that he may not be unwilling to bear every adversity for the sake of his friend.

62. There is nothing more praiseworthy in friendship than loyalty, which seems to be its nurse and guardian. It proves itself a true companion in all things—adverse and prosperous, joyful and sad, pleasing and bitter—beholding with the same eye the humble and the lofty, the poor and the rich, the strong and the weak, the healthy and the infirm. A truly loyal friend sees nothing in his friend but his heart. Embracing virtue in its proper place, and putting aside all else as if it were outside him, the faithful friend does not value them much if they are present, and does not seek them if they are absent. 63. Moreover, loyalty is hidden in prosperity, but conspicuous in adversity. A friend is tested in necessity.[45] The rich man's friends abound,[46] but whether they are true friends, intervening adversity proves. Solomon says: "He that is a friend loves at all times, and a brother is proved in distress."[47] And rebuking infidelity he says: "To trust an unfaithful man in the time of trouble is like a rotten tooth and weary foot."[48]

64. *Gratian.* But if no adversity ever spoils our prosperity, how will the loyalty of a friend be proved?

65. *Aelred.* There are many other ways in which the fidelity of a friend is proved, though ill fortune is the best. For, as we have said before, there is nothing which wounds friendship more than the betrayal of one's secret counsels. Indeed, the Gospel sentence reads: "He that is faithful in that which is little, will be faithful in that which is great."[49] Therefore, to those friends, for whom thus far we have thought probation necessary, we ought not confide to them all our profound secrets, but at first, external or little things about which one does not care a great deal whether they be concealed or exposed; yet this should be done with very great caution as if these smaller matters should do harm if betrayed, but would be of service if concealed. 66. If your friend has been found faithful in these smaller matters, do not hesitate to test him in greater. But if rumor chance to spread anything harmful about you, if anyone through malice has injured your reputation, and your friend believes nothing of these tales, is moved by no suspicion, and is disturbed by no doubt, you should have no further hesitation concerning his loyalty, but be very happy at having a friend who is safe and stable.

67. *Gratian.* Just now I call to mind that friend of yours across the sea,[50] whom you have often mentioned to us, the one whom you proved the truest and most faithful friend by a test of this kind. When certain individuals bore false witness against you, he not only did not relinquish his faith in you, but was not moved by any hesitation whatsoever; something you did not think you could presume upon even from your dearest friend, the old sacristan of Clairvaux.[51] But since we have said enough on the test of loyalty, proceed to explain the remaining points.

68. *Aelred.* We have said that the intention, too, should be proved. This is especially necessary, for there are very many who recognize nothing as good in human affairs, except what bears fruit in time. Such men love their friends as they do their cattle, from which they hope to derive some good.[52] They, indeed, lack genuine and spiritual friendship, which ought to be sought on account of God and for its own sake, they do not reflect upon the natural exemplar of love where the power of friendship may easily be detected both as to its quality and its greatness.[53] 69. Our Lord and Savior himself has written for us the formula of true friendship when he said: "You shall love your

neighbor as yourself."[54] Behold the mirror. You love yourself. Yes, especially if you love God, if you are such a person as we have described as worthy of being chosen for friendship. But tell me, do you think you should expect any reward from yourself for this love of yours? No, indeed, not the least, for from the very nature of things each one is dear to himself. Unless, therefore, you transfer his same affection to the other, loving him gratuitously, in that from the very nature of things in himself your friend seems dear, you cannot savor what true friendship is. 70. For then truly he whom you love will be another self, if you have transformed your love of self to him.[55] "For friendship is not tribute," as St. Ambrose says, "but a thing full of beauty, full of grace. It is a virtue, not a trade, because it is bought with love, not money, because it is acquired by competition in generosity, not by a haggling over its prices."[56] Therefore the intention of the one whom you have chosen must subtly be tested, that he may not wish to be joined in friendship to you according to the hope of some advantage, thinking friendship mercenary and not gratuitous.

Moreover, friendships among the poor are generally more secure than those among the rich,[57] since poverty takes away the hope of gain in such a way as not to decrease the love of friendship but rather to increase it. 71. And so towards the wealthy one acts flatteringly, but towards the poor no one pretends to be other than he is. Whatever is given to a poor man is a true gift, for the friendship of the poor is devoid of envy. We have made these statements that we may prove the character of our friends, not that we may appraise their financial rating. In this way, then, is intention proved. Should you see that your friend is more desirous of your goods than of yourself, always lying in wait for something which can be gained for himself through your effort: honor, glory, riches, freedom. If, in these matters, some worthier person is preferred to him, and especially if the object of his quest is not in your power, under these circumstances you will easily perceive with what intention he clings to you.

72. And now let us examine the quality of discretion. There are some men who are so perverse, not to say shameless,[58] as to wish a friend to be in character what they themselves cannot be. These are they who also bear impatiently the petty faults of their friends and rebuke them severely; and who, lacking discretion, neglect important matters but are aroused at all minute points. They confuse everything without regarding the fitting place, the due season, not the person to

whom one may fittingly reveal something, or from whom such matters must be concealed. For this reason, the discretion of him whom you choose should be proved, lest, if you associate with yourself in friendship anyone thoughtless or imprudent, you gain for yourself daily controversies and quarrels. 73. Indeed, it is easy enough to see that this virtue is necessary in friendship, since, if anyone lacks it, he is like a ship bereft of its pilot, borne along by every shifting and irrational movement. Many situations cannot fail to be at hand for a trying of the patience of him whom you desire as a friend, for you must needs rebuke him whom you love, and sometimes it is well, as it were, purposely to do this more severely, in order that the patience of your friend may be tested or tried.[59] 74. This certainly must be noted, that, although such faults as offend the soul be found in him whom you are proving, be they in the thoughtless revelation of some confidence, or the desire of some temporal gain, or a somewhat indiscreet rebuke, or overpassing the bounds of due gentleness, do not withdraw immediately from your proposed love or choice, as long as any hope of correction appears. And let no one in choosing or testing friends weary of being solicitous, since the fruit of this labor is the medicine of life and the most solid foundation of immortality.[60] 75. For since many men are experts in multiplying treasures and in feeding, choosing and comparing oxen and asses, and sheep and goats, and certain signs for recognition in all these matters are not lacking, it is madness not to give the same unwearied attention to acquiring and testing friends, and to learning certain marks whereby those whom we have chosen as friends may be proved suitable for friendship.[61] But surely a certain impulse of love should be guarded against, which runs ahead of judgment and takes away the power of testing. 76. Accordingly it is the part of the prudent man to pause, to hold in check this impulse,[62] to moderate his good will, and to proceed gradually in affection until he may give himself up wholly and commit himself to his now proven friend.

Dwelling in Friendship

- Have you ever tested someone with whom you hoped to become friends? If so, what did you test him or her for? Did you test them for any of the qualities on Aelred's list: loyalty, right intention, discretion, and patience? Have you yourself ever felt you were being tested by someone as a possible friend? If so, how did you feel? Was it a pleasant experience? Did it create any tension or anxiety in you?

Book Three: 76–87

✢

Introduction

When Walter states that it is probably better to live without friends, Aelred replies that without friends it is impossible to be happy (no. 76). We cannot enjoy anything in this life without the gift of companionship. Without friends, all riches, delights, honors, and possessions have no meaning and bring little, if any, joy (nos. 77–78). God has created the world in such a way that people have the capacity to befriend and love each other. True and eternal friendship begins in this life and is perfected in the next. Probation is necessary in friendship in this life because there is still a mixture of the wise and unwise. In the next life, however, there will be no need for probation, since it will already have blossomed into the fullness of perfection (nos. 79–80). A person without friends lives in constant fear and suspicion of others; the one with friends is most fortunate, for he rests in the hearts of others and experiences love and tranquility (no. 81).

Aelred admits to Walter and Gratian that it is difficult to find true and eternal friendship in the present life, but says that the more we develop such friendships, the happier we become (no. 82). He marvels at how wonderful it is to live in harmony with his brothers and cites St. Ambrose that a friend lays bare his heart to a friend and allows him to do likewise (no. 83). Walter then claims that Aelred's description of friendship is too sublime and that he prefers Augustine's description of friendship as conversing, reading, jesting, and many other activities that unite people and make them one in heart and mind (nos. 85–86). Aelred responds that such friendship is of the carnal type found especially among the young and may develop into something loftier and holier with the passage of time (no. 87).

✢

Text

76.

[*Walter, cont.*] I confess that I am still moved by the opinion of those men who think they live more safely without friends of this type.

Aelred. This is astonishing, since without friends absolutely no life can be happy.[63]

Walter. Why, I ask you?

77. *Aelred.* Let us imagine that the whole human race has been taken out of the world leaving you as the sole survivor. Now behold before you all the delights and riches of the world—gold, silver, precious stones, walled cities, turreted camps, spacious buildings, sculptures, and paintings.[64] And consider yourself also as transformed to that ancient state, having all creatures under your dominion, "all sheep and oxen; moreover, the beasts of the fields, the birds of the air, and the fishes of the sea that pass through the paths of the sea."[65] Tell me, now, whether without a companion you could enjoy all these possessions?

Walter. No, not at all.

78. *Aelred.* But suppose there were one person, whose language you did not know, of whose customs you were ignorant, whose love and heart lay concealed from you?

Walter. If I could not by some signs make him a friend, I should prefer to have no one at all rather than to have such a one.

Aelred. If, however, one were at hand whom you loved as much as yourself and by whom you were similarly loved, would not all these possessions, which before seemed bitter, become sweet and full of savor?

Walter. Indeed, they would.

Aelred. Would you not think yourself happier in proportion to the number of such companions?

Walter. By all means.

79. *Aelred.* This is that extraordinary and great happiness which we await, with God himself acting and diffusing, between himself and his creatures whom he has uplifted, among the very degrees and orders which he has distinguished, among the individual souls whom he has chosen, so much friendship and charity, that thus each loves another as he does himself; and that, by this means, just as each one rejoices in his own, so does he rejoice in the good fortune of another, and thus

the happiness of each one individually is the happiness of all, and the universality of all happiness is the possession of each individual. 80. There one finds no hiding of thoughts, no dissembling of affection. This is true and eternal friendship, which begins in this life and is perfected in the next, which here belongs to the few where few are good, but there belongs to all where all are good. Here, probation is necessary since there is a mingling of wise and unwise; there they need no probation, since an angelic and, in a certain manner, divine perfection beatifies them. To this pattern, then, let us compare our friends, whom we are to love as we do ourselves, whose confidences are to be laid bare to us, to whom our confidences are likewise to be disclosed, who are to be firm and stable and constant in all things. Do you think there is any human being who does not wish to be loved?[66]

Walter. I think not.

81. *Aelred.* If you were to see a man living among many people, suspecting all and fearing all as plotters against his own life, cherishing no one and thinking himself cherished by none, would you not judge such a man most wretched?[67]

Walter. Yes, very evidently so.

Aelred. Therefore you will not deny that he is most fortunate who rests in the inmost hearts of those among whom he lives, loving all and being loved by all,[68] whom neither suspicion severs nor fear cuts off from this sweetest tranquility.[69]

Walter. Excellently said, and most truly.

82. *Aelred.* But, perhaps, it is difficult to find this perfection with respect to all in this present life, since that is reserved for us in the life to come, yet shall we not consider ourselves happier in proportion as more individuals of this type abound for us?

The day before yesterday, as I was walking the round of the cloister of the monastery, the brethren were sitting around forming as it were a most loving crown. In the midst, as it were, of the delights of paradise with the leaves, flowers, and fruits of each single tree, I marveled. In that multitude of brethren I found no one whom I did not love, and no one by whom, I felt sure, I was not loved. I was filled with such joy that it surpassed all the delights of this world. I felt, indeed, my spirit transfused into all and the affection of all to have passed into me, so that I could say with the Prophet: "Behold, how good and how pleasant it is for brethren to dwell together in unity."[70]

Gratian. Are we not to think that you have taken into your friendship all those whom you thus love and by whom you are so loved?

83. *Aelred.* We embrace very many with every affection, but yet in such a way that we do not admit them to the secrets of friendship, which consists especially in the revelation of all our confidences and plans. Whence it is that the Lord in the Gospel says: "I will not now call you servants but friends";[71] and then adding the reason for which they are considered worthy of the name of friend: "because all things, whatsoever I have heard of my Father, I have made known to you."[72] And in another place: "You are my friends, if you do the things that I command you."[73] From these words, as Saint Ambrose says, "He gives the formula of friendship for us to follow: namely, that we do the will of our friend, that we disclose to our friend whatever confidences we have in our hearts, and that we be not ignorant of his confidences. Let us lay bare to him our heart and let him disclose his to us. For a friend hides nothing. If he is true, he pours forth his soul just as the Lord Jesus poured forth the mysteries of the Father."[74] 84. Thus speaks Ambrose. How many, therefore, do we love before whom it would be imprudent to lay bare our souls and pour out our inner hearts! Men whose age or feeling or discretion is not sufficient to bear such revelations.

85. *Walter.* This friendship is so sublime and perfect that I dare not aspire to it. For me and our friend Gratian that type of friendship suffices which your Augustine describes: namely, to converse and jest together, with good will to humor one another, to read together, to discuss matters together, together to trifle, and together to be in earnest; to differ at times without ill humor, as a man would do with himself, and even by a very infrequent disagreement to give zest to our very numerous agreements; to teach one another something, or to learn from one another; with impatience to long for one another when absent, and with joy to receive one another when returning. 86. By these and similar indications emanating from the hearts of those who love and are loved in turn, through the countenance, the tongue, the eyes, and a thousand pleasing movements, to fuse our spirits by tinder, as it were, and out of many to make but one. This is what we think we should love in our friends, so that our conscience will be its own accuser, if we have not loved him who in turn loves us, or if we have not returned love to him who first loved us.[75]

87. *Aelred.* This type of friendship belongs to the carnal, and especially to the young people, such as they once were, Augustine and the friend of whom he was then speaking. And yet this friendship except for trifles and deceptions, if nothing dishonorable enters into it, is to be tolerated in the hope of more abundant grace, as the beginnings, so to say, of a holier friendship.[76] By these beginnings, with a growth in piety and in constant zeal for things of the spirit, with the growing seriousness of mature years and the illumination of the spiritual senses,[77] they may, with purer affections, mount to loftier heights from, as it were, a region close by, just as yesterday we said that the friendship of man could be easily translated into a friendship for God himself because of the similarity existing between both.

Dwelling in Friendship

- How important are friendships to you? Do you see them as a basic necessity of life? Like Walter, have you ever thought that they are too much trouble and that you would be better off without them? Can you imagine your life without friends? Is it possible to have too many friends? Do you agree with Aelred that the more true friends we have in life the happier we become? Do you aspire toward the highest form of friendship or are you willing to settle for something less?

Book Three: 88–97

Introduction

At this point in their conversation, Aelred says it is time to examine precisely how spiritual friendship should be cultivated. He states that loyalty is the foundation of friendship and such qualities as stability, constancy, frankness, congeniality, and sympathy should be fostered among friends (no. 88). Suspicion should be avoided at all costs. We should not think evil of a friend, but instead foster a sense of trust that allows a sense of affability, congeniality, relaxation, and ease in one another's presence (no. 89). He goes on to say that friends should relate to one another as equals and that it is therefore necessary for those of a higher station to descend and those of a lower one to ascend or be lifted up (nos. 90–91). He cites the friendship between Jonathan and David as an example from scripture that substantiates this claim (nos. 92–95). He offers a description of true friendship and again quotes from St. Ambrose to emphasize the importance of maintaining equality in a friendship (nos. 96–97).

Text

88. *[Aelred, cont.].* But now it is time that we examine the points, one after another, as to how friendship is to be cultivated. Loyalty, then, is the foundation of stability and constancy in friendship, for nothing is stable that is unfaithful.[78] Indeed, the frank, the congenial, and the sympathetic, and those who can be stirred by like qualities, ought to be friends to one another; and all of these qualities pertain to fidelity.[79] For a changeable and crafty character cannot be faithful, nor can those who have not like interests and mutual agreements on like matters be stable or faithful in friendship.

89. Above all things, however, suspicion ought to be avoided, for it is the poison of friendship. Let us never think evil regarding a friend, or believe or agree with anyone speaking evil of our friend. And here let us add affability in speech, cheerfulness of countenance, suavity in manners, serenity in the expression of the eyes, matters in which there is to be found no slight relish to friendship.[80] For sadness and a rather severe demeanor give one a certain appearance of gravity, but friendship ought to be, so to say, rather relaxed at times; it ought to be somewhat free and mild, and rather incline to congeniality and easiness of approach without levity and dissipation.[81]

90. It is also a law of friendship that a superior must be on a plane of equality with the inferior.[82] For often, indeed, persons of inferior rank or order of dignity or knowledge are assumed into friendship by persons of greater excellence. In this case it behooves them to despise and esteem as nothing and as vanity what is but an addition to nature, and always to direct their attention to the beauty of friendship, which is not adorned with silken garments or gems, is not expanded by possessions, does not grow fat with delicacies, does not abound in riches, is not exalted by honors, is not puffed up by dignities. Coming back to the principle of friendship's origin, let them consider with care the quality which nature has given, rather than the external trappings which avarice affords to human kind.

91. Therefore in friendship, which is the perfect gift of nature and grace alike, let the lofty descend, the lowly ascend; the rich be in want, the poor become rich; and thus let each communicate his condition to the other, so that equality may be the result. Hence it is written: "He that had much, had nothing over; and he that had little, had no want."[83] Never, therefore, prefer yourself to your friend; but if you chance to find yourself the superior in those things which we have mentioned, then do not hesitate to abase yourself before your friend, to give him your confidence, to praise him if he is shy, and to confer honor upon him in inverse proportion to that warranted by his lowliness and poverty.[84]

92. Jonathan, that excellent youth, paying no heed to a royal crown or to the hope of regal power, entered upon a covenant with David.[85] He made the servant, David, an equal in friendship in the Lord. He preferred him to himself, when David was driven into flight before Saul, when he was hiding in the desert, when he was condemned to death, when he was destined for slaughter; thus Jonathan humiliated

himself and exalted his friend. "You," he said, "shall be king, and I will be next after you."[86] O mirror most excellent of true friendship! Marvel of marvels! The king was enraged against his servant, and was arousing the entire country against him as one emulous of his power. Accusing the priests of treachery, he was slaying them for mere suspicion. He rages through the woods, searches the valleys, and encompasses mountains and cliffs with an armed band, while all pledge themselves vindicators of the royal wrath; Jonathan only, who alone could be somewhat justifiably envious, thought it proper to oppose his father, to defer to his friend, and to offer him counsel in the face of his opposition. Preferring friendship to a kingdom, "You," he said, "shall be king, and I will be next after you."[87]

93. And see how Saul, the father of the youth, strove to arouse envy in him against his friend, heaping him with reproaches, terrifying him with threats, reminding Jonathan that he would be despoiled of a kingdom and deprived of honor. But when Saul had uttered the sentence of death against David, Jonathan did not fail his friend. "Why shall David die? Wherein has he sinned? What has he done? He put his life in his hands, and slew the Philistine, and you rejoiced. Why, therefore, shall he die?"[88] At this utterance the king became angered and strove to nail Jonathan to the wall with his spear; and adding reproaches to threats, he said: "You son of a woman that is the ravisher of a man, I know that you love him to your own confusion and to the confusion of your shameless mother!"[89]

94. Then he spewed out poison to steep the heart of the youth, adding the word that was an inducement to ambition, a ferment of envy, an incentive to emulousness and bitterness: "As long as the son of Jesse lives, your kingdom will not be established."[90] Who would not be stirred by these words, who would not be made envious? Whose love, whose favors, whose friendship would these words not corrupt, nor diminish, nor obliterate? That most loving youth, preserving the laws of friendship, brave in the face of threats, patient before reproaches, despising a kingdom because of his friendship, unmindful of glory, but mindful of grace, declared: "You shall be king, and I will be next after you."[91]

95. Tullius says that some have been found who think it mean to prefer money to friendship; but that it is impossible to discover those who do not put honors, civic offices, military commands, power or riches before friendship; so that when these sentiments are offered

on the one hand, and the claims of friendship on the other, they will much prefer the former. For nature is too weak to despise power.[92] "For where," he says, "will you find one who prefers the honor of his friend to his own?"[93] Behold, Jonathan was found a victor over nature, a despiser of glory and of power, one who preferred the honor of his friend to his own, saying: "You shall be king, and I will be next after you."[94]

96. This is true, perfect, constant, and eternal friendship; which envy does not corrupt, nor suspicion diminish, nor ambition dissolve; which thus tempted does not yield, thus assailed does not fall; which is perceived to be unyielding though struck by reproaches innumerable and though wounded by injuries manifold. Therefore, "go and do you in like manner."[95] But if you think it hard and even impossible to prefer him whom you love to yourself, do not fail at least to hold him on an equal footing with yourself if you wish to be a friend.

97. For they do not rightly develop friendship who do not preserve equality. "Defer to your friend as to an equal," says Ambrose, "and be not ashamed to anticipate a friend in a service. For friendship knows no pride. Indeed, a faithful friend is the medicine of life,[96] the charm of immortality."[97]

Dwelling in Friendship

- Have you found Aelred's use of scriptural examples helpful in understanding his teaching on friendship? Does his use of the relationship between David and Jonathan, for example, demonstrate what it means to be loyal, well intentioned, discrete, and patient in a friendship? What can examples and images accomplish that words and concepts cannot? Have you ever had a friend who was as close to you as Jonathan was to David? Do you wish you did?

Book Three: 97–110

✜

Introduction

A t this point, Aelred turns his attention to how we should foster our relationship with those we have finally befriended. Citing Cicero, he says that we should seek only what is honorable from friends, and that we should do only what is honorable in return (no. 97). Friends should offer themselves and their goods for each other and even anticipate each other's needs (nos. 98-99). They should do so, moreover, in such a way that the giver remains in good cheer and the one who receives maintains his confidence (no. 99). He cites the generosity of Boaz toward Ruth the Moabite as a Scriptural example of how friends should anticipate the needs of their friends and preserve their dignity (no. 100). Walter wonders what such a principle would mean for those in the monastery who are not permitted to give and receive gifts (no. 100). Aelred responds that the vow of poverty strengthens friendship, for once friendship is purified of the burden of the desire for material goods, it is free to deal in the giving and receiving of spiritual resources such as caring for, praying for, rejoicing with, and grieving for one another (no. 101). A friend should regard a friend's progress as his own and do nothing that is dishonorable or unbecoming (nos. 101-2). Friends need to nurture a mutual respect for each other (no. 102). Counsel, when needed, is often more readily received and retained from a friend (no. 103). When a friend errs, he should be admonished, even reproved if necessary (no. 104). Again he cites St. Ambrose, this time on the importance of correcting an erring friend (no. 106). We should always have the betterment of our friend at heart and avoid anger and bitterness when admonishing him. We must speak the truth to our friend, and there should be no hesitation or pretense between us (nos. 108-9). True friendship will delay correcting a friend for a good reason (dissimilation), but will never completely forgo it simply to preserve a false and tenuous peace (simulation) (no. 109).

✜

Text

97. *[Aelred, cont.].* And now let us devote our attention to the question of how the benefits of friendship are to be cultivated; and on this topic let us wrest some information from other's hands. "Let this law," someone says, "be established with respect to friendship, that we seek what is honorable from our friends, and ourselves perform what is honorable for them, and let us not wait to be asked. Let there never be any delay in a friend's service!"[98]

98. If we must be prepared to lose money on our friends, how much more ought we be prepared to give it to them when their advantage or their need requires it? But not all can do everything. One abounds in money, another in lands and goods; one can effect more by counsel, and still another excels in dignity of office. But in these matters consider prudently how you must conduct yourself toward your friend. And concerning money, Scripture has given ample advice: "Lose your money for your friend."[99] But as the "eyes of the wise man are in his head," let us, if we are the members and Christ the head,[100] act according to the words of the Prophet: "My eyes are ever toward the Lord";[101] so that we may receive our manner of life from the Lord, concerning which it is written: "If any want wisdom, let him ask to God, who gives to all men abundantly, and does not upbraid."[102]

99. Therefore, give to your friend in such a way that you do not reproach him, or expect a reward. Do not wrinkle your brow, or turn aside your countenance or avert your eyes; but with a serene countenance, a cheerful aspect and pleasing speech, anticipate the request of him who is seeking a favor. Meet him with kindness, so that you may appear to be granting his request without being asked.[103] The sensitive soul thinks nothing more worthy of a blush than to beg. Since, therefore, you and your friend ought to be of one heart and one soul,[104] it is unjust, if there is not also but one purse. Let this law, therefore, be held in this respect among friends, namely, that they expend themselves and their goods for one another in such a way that he who gives preserves a cheerful aspect, and that he who receives does not lose confidence.

100. When Boaz observed the poverty of Ruth, the Moabite, he spoke to her as she was gathering ears of corn behind his reapers, consoled her and invited her to the table of his servants, and sparing

in kindly fashion her embarrassment, he ordered his reapers to leave ears of corn even purposely so that she might collect them without shame.[105] In the same way we ought the more adroitly seek out the needs of our friends, anticipate their requests by good services, and observe such demeanor in our giving that the recipient, rather than the giver, appears to be bestowing the favor.

Walter. But for us, who are permitted to receive nothing and to bestow nothing, what will be the charm of spiritual friendship in this respect?

101. *Aelred.* Men would lead a very happy life, says the Wise Man, if these two words were taken from their midst: namely, "mine" and "yours."[106] For holy poverty certainly bestows great strength upon spiritual friendship, poverty which is holy for the reason that it is voluntary. For since cupidity makes heavy demands on friendship, friendship once attained is the more easily preserved in proportion as the soul is found more fully purified of this pest. There are, moreover, other resources in spiritual love, by means of which friends can be of aid and advantage to one another. The first is to be solicitous for one another, to pray for one another, to blush for one another, to rejoice for one another, to grieve for one another's fall as one's own, to regard another's progress as one's own.

102. By whatever means are in one's power, one ought to raise the weak, support the infirm, console the afflicted, restrain the wrathful. Furthermore one ought so to respect the eye of a friend as to dare to do nothing which is dishonorable, or dare to say nothing which is unbecoming. For when one fails one's self in anything, the act ought so to well over to one's friend, that the sinner not only blushes and grieves within himself, but that even the friend who sees or hears reproaches himself as if he himself has sinned. In fact, the friend will believe that he deserves no compassion, but that his erring associate does. Therefore, the best companion of friendship is reverence, and so he who deprives friendship of respect takes away its greatest adornment.[107]

103. How often has the nod of my friend restrained or extinguished the flame of anger aroused within me and already bursting forth into public gaze! How frequently his rather severe demeanor has repressed the unbecoming word already on my lips! How often when carelessly breaking into laughter, or lapsing into idleness, I have recovered a proper dignity at his approach! Besides, whatever counsel is to be given

is more easily received from a friend, and more steadfastly retained, for a friend's power in counseling must needs be great,[108] since there can neither be doubt of his loyalty nor suspicion of flattery.

104. Therefore, let friend counsel friend as to what is right, securely, openly, and freely. And friends are not only to be admonished, but if necessity arise, reproved as well. For although truth is offensive to some, seeing that hatred is born of it according to the aphorism: "Compliance begets friends, truth gives birth to hatred";[109] yet that complacency is by far more hurtful, because it indulges in wrongdoing and thus suffers a friend to be borne along headlong to ruin.[110] However, that friend is more grievously culpable and therefore especially to be reproached if he scorns truth and by complaisances and blandishments is driven to crime. Not that we ought not kindly to honor our friends and often praise them. But in all things moderation must be preserved, so that admonition be without bitterness, and reproof be without incentive.

105. Indeed, in humoring and praising let there be a certain kind and honorable friendliness; but let subserviency, the helpmate of vices, be far removed as a thing unworthy, not only of a friend, but even of any free-born person. Moreover, if a man's ears are so closed to the truth that he is not able to hear the truth from a friend, his salvation must be despaired of.[111]

106. Therefore, as Saint Ambrose says, "if you perceive any vice in your friend, correct him secretly; if he will not listen to you, correct him openly. For corrections are good and often better than a friendship which holds its peace. And even though your friend think himself wronged, nevertheless correct him. Even though the bitterness of correction wound his soul, nevertheless cease not to correct him. For the wounds inflicted by a friend are more tolerable than the kisses of flatterers.[112] Therefore, correct the erring friend."[113]

And yet, above all things, one ought to avoid anger and bitterness of spirit in correction, that he may be seen to have the betterment of his friend at heart rather than the satisfaction of his own ill humor.

107. For I have seen some, in correcting their friends, clothe with the name now of zeal, now of liberty, the bitterness within them and their outsurging rage; and because they follow impulse rather than reason, they never effect any good by such correction, but rather cause harm. But among friends there is no excuse for this vice. For a friend ought to sympathize with a friend, he ought to condescend, to think

of his friend's fault as his own, to correct him humbly and sympatheti-
cally. Let a somewhat troubled countenance make the reproof, as also
a saddened utterance; let tears interrupt words, so that the other may
not only see but even feel that the reproof proceeds from love rather
than from rancor. If he chance to have rejected the first correction,
let him receive even a second. Meanwhile, pray and weep, displaying a
troubled countenance, but preserving a holy affection.

108. One ought even to study the disposition of his heart. For
there are those with whom coaxings are effective, and such persons
quite readily assent thereto. There are others who are impervious to
coaxing, and are more easily corrected by a word or a blow. Let a man,
therefore, conform and adapt himself to his friend to be in harmony
with his disposition. As one ought to be of aid to a friend in his material setbacks, so he ought the more readily hasten to succour him in
trials of the spirit. It is characteristic of friendship to admonish and to
be admonished, and to do the former freely, not harshly, and to receive
the latter patiently, not resentfully; so it should be understood that in
friendship there is no greater pest than flattery and subserviency,[114]
which are the marks of fickle and deceitful men, who speak everything
at the whim of another, but speak nothing with an eye to truth.

109. Accordingly, let there be no hesitation among friends, and
no pretense, a thing most of all repugnant to friendship. Indeed, a
man owes truth to his friend, without which the name of friendship
has no value.[115] "The just man," says holy David, "shall correct me in
mercy, and shall reprove me; but let not the oil of the sinner fatten my
head."[116] The pretender and the man of cunning provoke the wrath
of God. Thus the Lord says through his Prophet: "O my people, they
that call you blessed, the same deceive you, and destroy the way of
your steps."[117] For, as Solomon says: "The dissembler with his mouth
deceives his friend."[118] Therefore, friendship ought so to be cultivated
that, although it may perhaps tolerate dissimulation for good reasons,
it will never tolerate simulation.

Walter. How, pray, can dissimulation be necessary, a thing which, so
it seems to me, is always a vice?

110. *Aelred.* You are mistaken, son, for God is said to dissimulate
in regard to the sins of the delinquent,[119] not wishing the death of the
sinner, but that he be converted, and live.[120]

Dwelling in Friendship

- Do you agree that we should ask from and do for a friend only what is honorable? If, so, how do we determine precisely what that may mean in a given situation? Do you believe that friends should not use the words "mine" and "yours?" Are there limits to the amount of material wealth we should share with our friends? Do you agree that friends have an obligation to correct one another? If so, when and how should this be done?

Book Three: 110–127

Introduction

Walter asks Aelred to distinguish between simulation and dissimulation (no. 110), and Aelred complies. Dissimulation is dispensing with or postponing a correction or punishment because of the circumstances of a particular situation (no. 112), while the simulation is a deceptive agreement that assents to everything regardless of the circumstances (no. 111). He cites the example from scripture of how the prophet Nathan's prudent manner of getting King David to accuse himself as a good example of dissimulation (no. 113).

Walter then asks if we should promote friends to high places when we find ourselves in a position of authority (no. 114). Aelred replies that we should do so with great caution (no. 115). We should be concerned not with the office or honor we are bestowing, but with what our friends can endure. We should also make sure that we follow what reason and not feeling tells us (no. 116). When not promoted, a friend should not feel hated or unloved (no. 117). Similarly, when in a position of authority, we should be satisfied with our friends as they are, and not feel obligated to bestow worthless honors on them (no. 118). Adding a more personal touch, Aelred then relates how he drew close to two of his friends and how each relationship possessed a different mixture of reason and affection. He then describes how he experienced the stages of friendship in them differently, how he dealt with questions relating to the bestowal of office regarding them, and how he experienced the depths of spiritual friendship through them (nos. 119–127).

Text

110. [*Walter, cont.*] Distinguish, please, between simulation and dissimulation.

111. *Aelred.* Simulation, I think, is a kind of deceptive agreement, opposed to the judgment of reason, which Terence, in the person of Gnatho, rather excellently expressed: "Does some one say 'no'? I say 'no'. Does one say, 'yes'? I say, 'yes' too. In fine, I have ordered myself to give assent in everything."[121] Perhaps that well-known pagan borrowed these ideas from our treasures, expressing the sentiment of our Prophet in his own words. For it is clear that the Prophet said this very thing in the person of the perverted people: "See errors for us, speak unto us pleasant things."[122] And in another place: "The prophets prophesied falsehood, and the priests clapped their hands; and my people loved such things."[123] This vice should be detested everywhere, always and everywhere it should be shunned.

112. Now, dissimulation is in a sense a dispensing with, or a putting off of punishment or correction, without interior approval, in consideration of place, time, or person.[124] For if a friend when he is in the midst of others should commit some fault, he should not suddenly and publicly be reproached; but one ought to "dissemble" because of the place, nay, further, as far as is compatible with truth, one ought to excuse what he has done, and wait to administer in secret the deserved rebuke. Likewise, at a time when the mind is engrossed in many considerations and so is less receptive of those matters which must be spoken, or, when, for other reasons that have intervened, the friend's feelings are a trifle more moved and he is, in consequence, somewhat disturbed—in both instances there is need of dissimulation until the tumult within has been calmed, and he can endure without irritation the needful correction.

113. When King David, yielding to lust, added murder to adultery, the prophet Nathan was sent to correct him. Deferential to his royal majesty, he did not suddenly nor with agitation of mind accuse so distinguished a personage of his crime, but using the shield of suitable dissimulation, he prudently extracted from the king himself a judgment against his own person.[125]

114. *Walter.* That distinction pleases me very much. But I should like to know whether a friend who has more power and is able to promote

whomsoever he wishes to honors and distinctions, ought to prefer to others in such promotions those whom he cherishes and by whom he is cherished; and, if so, whether he ought among his friends to give precedence to those whom he loves with greater predilection?[126]

115. *Aelred.* In regard to this point it is to our advantage to examine how friendship is to be cultivated. For there are some persons who think they are not loved because they cannot be promoted, and who allege that they are despised, if they are not entrusted with responsibilities and offices. We know that as a result of this type of thinking no small discord has sprung up among those who were considered friends, so that estrangement followed upon indignation, and railings upon estrangement. Thus great caution must be observed in the conferring of dignities and offices, especially ecclesiastical ones. You should not be concerned about what you are able to bestow, but rather about what he, upon whom you bestow anything, can endure.

116. Indeed, many are to be loved, who, nevertheless, should not be advanced to office; and we happily and laudably embrace many whom we could not involve in responsibilities and undertakings without grave sin on our part and great danger on theirs. Therefore, in these matters one should always be guided by reason and not by affection. A dignity and burden of office should not be imposed on those whom we prefer as friends, but rather on those whom we believe better suited to sustain such dignities and burdens. Where, however, equality of virtue is found, I do not greatly disapprove if to some degree affection gives play to its feelings.[127]

117. Nor should anyone say that he is held in contempt for the reasons that he is not promoted, since the Lord Jesus preferred Peter to John in this respect; nor did he, on that account, lessen his affection for John, because he had given Peter the leadership.[128] To Peter he commended his Church; to John, his most beloved Mother.[129] To Peter he gave the keys of his kingdom;[130] to John he revealed the secrets of his heart. Peter, therefore, was the more exalted;[131] John, the more secure. Although Peter was established in power, nevertheless when Jesus said, "One of you will betray me," he was afraid and trembled along with the rest; but John, leaning on the bosom of his Master, was made the bolder, and at a nod from Peter asked who the traitor was.[132] Peter, therefore, was exposed to action, John was reserved for love, according to the words of Christ: "So will I have him remain till I come."[133] Thus Christ gave us the example that we might do in like manner.[134]

118. Let us afford our friend whatever love, whatever kindness, whatever sweetness, whatever charity we can; but let us impose vain honors and burdens on those who, reason dictates, should be burdened, realizing that a man never truly loves a friend if he is not satisfied with his friend as he is, but must needs add these worthless and contemptible honors. One must also greatly guard against permitting a too tender affection from hindering greater utility.[135] This would be the case were we unwilling to part from or to burden those whom we embrace in greater charity then great hope of more abundant fruit is to be realized. For this is well-ordered friendship, namely, that reason rules affection, and that we attend more to the general welfare than to our friend's good humor.[136]

119. I recall now two friends, who, although they have passed from this present life, nevertheless live to me and always will so live.[137] The first of these I gained as my friend when I was still young, in the beginning of my conversion, because of a certain resemblance between us in character and similarity of interests;[138] the other I chose when he was still a boy, and after I had tested him repeatedly in various ways, when at length age was silvering my hair, I admitted him into my most intimate friendship.[139] Indeed, I chose the former as my companion, as the one who shared in the delights of the cloister and the spiritual joys which I was just beginning to taste when I, too, was not as yet burdened with any pastoral duty or perplexed with temporal affairs. I demanded nothing and I bestowed nothing but affection and the loving judgment of affection itself according as charity dictated. The latter I claimed when he was still young to be a sharer in my anxieties and a co-worker in these labors of mine. Looking back, as far as my memory permits, upon each of these friendships, I see that the first rested for the most part on affection and the second on reason, although affection was not lacking in the latter, or reason in the former.

120. In fine, my first friend, taken from me in the very beginnings of our friendship, I was able to choose, as I have said, but not to test; the other, devoted to me from boyhood even to middle age, and loved by me, mounted with me through all the stages of friendship, as far as human imperfection permitted. And, indeed, it was my admiration for his virtues that first directed my affection toward him, and it was I who long ago brought him from the South to this northern solitude, and first introduced him to regular discipline. From that time he learned to conquer his own flesh and to endure labor and hunger;[140]

to very many he was an example, to many a source of admiration, and
to myself a source of honor and delight. Already at that time I thought
that he should be nurtured in the beginnings of friendship, seeing
that he was a burden to no one but pleasing to all.

121. He came and went, hastening at the command of his superi-
ors, humble, gentle, reserved in manner, sparing of speech, a stranger
to indignation, and unacquainted with murmuring, rancor, and
detraction; he walked "as one deaf, hearing not, and as one dumb,
not opening his mouth."[141] "He became as a beast of burden,"[142]
submissive to the reins of obedience, and bearing untiringly the yoke
of regular discipline in mind and body. Once when he was still young
he was in the infirmary and he was rebuked by my holy father and
predecessor[143] for yielding so early in life to rest and inactivity. The
boy was so ashamed at this that he immediately left the infirmary and
subjected himself with such zeal to corporal labor that for many years
he would not allow himself any relaxation from his accustomed rigor,
even when he was afflicted with serious illness.[144]

122. All this in a most wondrous way had bound him to me by
the most intimate bonds, and had so brought him into my affection,
that from an inferior I made him my companion, from a companion
a friend, from a friend my most cherished of friends.[145] For when I saw
that he had advanced far in the life of virtue and grace, I consulted
the brethren and imposed upon him the burden of subpriorship. This
burden, against his will, to be sure, but because he had vowed himself
to obedience, he modestly accepted. Yet he pleaded with me in secret
to be relieved of it, alleging as excuse his age, his lack of knowledge,
and finally the friendship which we had but lately formed, fearful that
this might prove to be an occasion for him either to love the less or to
be loved the less.[146]

123. But, availing nothing by these entreaties, then he began to
reveal quite freely but at the same time humbly and modestly what
he feared for each of us, and what in me pleased him but little. He
hoped thereby, as he afterwards confessed, that I would be offended
by this presumption, and would the more easily be inclined to grant
his request. But his freedom of speech and spirit only led our friendship to its culmination, for my desire for his friendship was lessened
not a whit. Perceiving then that his words had pleased me, and that
I answered humbly to each accusation and had satisfied him in all
these matters, and that he himself had not only caused no offense but

rather had received more fruitful benefit, he began to manifest his love for me even more ardently than theretofore, to relax the reins of his affection,[147] and to reveal himself wholly to my heart. In this way we tested one another, I making proof of his freedom of utterance and he of my patience.

124. And I, too, repaid my friend in kind in his turn. Thinking that I should at an opportune moment harshly reprove him, I did not spare him any, as it were, reproaches, and I found him patient with my frankness and grateful. Then I began to reveal to him the secrets of my innermost thoughts, and I found him faithful. In this way love increased between us, affection glowed the warmer and charity was strengthened, until we attained that stage at which we had but one mind and one soul[148] to will and not to will alike,[149] and at which our love was devoid of fear and ignorant of offense, shunning suspicion and abhorring flattery.

125. There was no pretense between us, no simulation, no dishonorable flattery, no unbecoming harshness, no evasion, no concealment, but everything open and above board; for I deemed my heart in a fashion his, and his mine, and he felt in like manner towards me. And so, as we were progressing in friendship without deviation, neither's correction evoked the indignation of the other, neither's yielding produced blame. Therefore, proving himself a friend in every respect, he provided as much as was in his power for my peace and my rest. He exposed himself to dangers and he forestalled scandals in their very inception.

126. Occasionally I wanted to provide him for his ailments with some alleviation from creature comforts, but he opposed it, saying that we should be on our guard against having our love measured according to the consolation of the flesh, and of having the gift be ascribed to my carnal affection rather than to his need, with the resultant effect that my authority might in consequence be diminished. He was, therefore, as it were, my hand, my eye,[150] the staff of my old age.[151] He was the refuge of my spirit, the sweet solace of my griefs, whose heart of love received me when fatigued from labors, whose counsel refreshed me when plunged in sadness and grief.

127. He himself calmed me when distressed, he soothed me when angry. Whenever anything unpleasant occurred, I referred it to him, so that, shoulder to shoulder, I was able to bear more easily what I could not bear alone. What more is there, then, that I can say? Was

it not a foretaste of blessedness thus to love and thus to be loved;[152] thus to help and thus to be helped; and in this way from the sweetness of fraternal charity to wing one's flight aloft to that more sublime splendor of divine love, and by the ladder of charity now to mount to the embrace of Christ himself; and again to descend to the love of neighbor, there pleasantly to rest? And so, in this friendship of ours, which we have introduced by way of example, if you see aught worthy of imitation, profit by it to advance your own perfection.

Dwelling in Friendship

- Do you think it is appropriate to postpone correcting our friends to avoid embarrassing them in front of others? Have you ever done so? Has anyone ever done so to you? Are there any viable alternatives to this kind of dissimulation? If you had the opportunity to promote a friend, would you do so automatically? What considerations would you keep in mind? Where would the good of your friend fit into your decision?

Book Three: 128–134

Introduction

Aelred concludes Book Three with a fitting summary of all that he has discussed with Walter and Gratian, and ends by giving us a sense of how spiritual friendship offers each friend the opportunity to come into close personal contact with Christ (nos. 128–134).

Text

128. *[Aelred, cont.].* But since it is growing late and we must at last close this discussion of ours, you are surely convinced that friendship is founded on love. Indeed, who is there that can love another, if he does not love himself since, from a comparison with that love by which he is dear to himself, a man ought to regulate his love for his neighbor. A man does not love himself who exacts of himself or commands from himself anything shameful or dishonorable.

129. In the first place, then, one must needs chastise one's self, allowing nothing which is unbecoming and refusing nothing which is profitable. And loving himself thus, let him follow the same rule in loving his neighbor.[153] But as this love includes many persons, let him choose from among them one whom he can admit in familiar fashion to the mysteries of friendship, and upon whom he can bestow his affection in abundance, laying bare his mind and heart even to their sinews and marrow, that is, even to the most secret thoughts and desires of the heart.

130. Let such a friend be chosen, moreover, not according to the caprice of affection but rather according to the foresight of reason, because of similarity of character and the contemplation of virtue.

Then let a man so attach himself to his friend that all levity be absent and all joy be present, and let there be no lack of proper services and courtesies of benevolence and charity. Next let the loyalty of your proposed friend be tested, as well as his honor and his patience. Let there gradually be added sharing of counsels, application to common concern and a certain conformity in outward expression.

131. For friends ought to be so alike that immediately upon seeing one another a likeness of expression is reflected from the first to the second, whether he be cast down by sorrow or serene with joy. After he has thus been chosen and tested, and when you are assured that he will wish to ask of a friend or to do himself if asked nothing that would be unbecoming; and moreover, when you are confident that he looks upon friendship as a virtue and not as a trade, and that he shuns flattery and detests obsequiousness; and finally, when you have discovered that he is frank, yet with discretion, patient under reproof, firm and constant in affection, then you will experience that spiritual delight, namely, "how good and how pleasant it is for brethren to dwell together in unity."[154]

132. How advantageous it is then to grieve for one another, to toil for one another, to bear one another's burdens,[155] while each considers it sweet to forget himself for the sake of the other, to prefer the will of the other to his own, to minister to the other's needs rather than one's own, to oppose and expose one's self to misfortunes! Meanwhile, how delightful friends find it to converse with one another, mutually to reveal their interests, to examine all things together, and to agree on all of them!

133. Added to this there is prayer for one another,[156] which, coming from a friend, is the more efficacious in proportion as it is more lovingly sent to God, with tears which either fear excites or affection awakens or sorrow evokes. And thus a friend praying to Christ on behalf of his friend, and for his friend's sake desiring to be heard by Christ, directs his attention with love and longing to Christ; then it sometimes happens that quickly and imperceptibly the one love passes over into the other, and coming, as it were, into close contact with the sweetness of Christ himself, the friend begins to taste his sweetness and to experience his charm.[157]

134. Thus ascending from that holy love with which he embraces a friend to that with which he embraces Christ, he will joyfully partake in abundance of the spiritual fruit of friendship, awaiting the fullness

of all things in the life to come. Then, with the dispelling of all anxiety by reason of which we now fear and are solicitous for one another, with the removal of all adversity which it now behooves us to bear for one another, and, above all, with the destruction of the sting of death together with death itself,[158] whose pangs now often trouble us and force us to grieve for one another, with salvation secured, we shall rejoice in the eternal possession of Supreme Goodness; and this friendship, to which here we admit but few, will be outpoured upon all and by all outpoured upon God, and God shall be all in all.[159]

Dwelling in Friendship

- Do you agree that friendship is founded on love and that we cannot love others if we do not first love ourselves? Do you believe that the love we have for ourselves should direct the way we love our friends? What is the difference between love of self and selfishness? Is it possible for us to love ourselves without the help of God? Is it possible for us to love others without the help of God? What, in your opinion, is the meaning of friendship in Christ?

Book Three Review

- Do you agree with Aelred's presentation of the four stages of friendship: selection, probation, admission, and perfect harmony in matters human and divine with charity and benevolence? What are the positive aspects of such a presentation? What are the negative? Does this teaching make sense today? Can you see yourself using such an approach in forming friendships with others? If not, why not?

- Do you agree with Aelred's list of the negative habits of thought and action that would disqualify a person for friendship? Is there anything you would add or detract from this list? Are any of these qualities more important than the others? What would your own list of negative traits to avoid in a friend look like? Do you see any of these negative qualities in any of your own friends? If so, how do you deal with them?

- Do you agree with Aelred's list of the positive habits of thought and action necessary for spiritual friendship? Is there anything you would add or detract from this list? Are any of these qualities more important than the others? What would your own list of positive traits to look for in a friend be like? To what extent are these traits present or absent in the people you have befriended in your life?

- Do you agree with Aelred and St. Jerome that true friendships last forever? Have you ever been in a relationship with someone whom you thought was a true friend, but was not? If so, how did you recognize the situation? How did you react to the person once you better understood the nature of your relationship to him or her? Do you agree with Aelred that such friendships should be unraveled "stitch-by-stitch" over an extended period of time? Have you ever tried this yourself?

- Why does Aelred go out of his way to cite examples from his own life when discussing the practical dimensions of spiritual friendship? Does it make him more credible? Does it strengthen his bond with his readers? Does it help you to better understand his teaching? Does it encourage you to look for concrete examples in your own life where the practical aspects of his teaching on spiritual friendship apply? Does such sharing change the nature of the treatise? How important is it for the formation of spiritual friendships?

Abbreviations

⁂

AMIC   Marcus Tullius Cicero, *On Friendship*, Tr. W. Falconer in *De Senectute—De Amicitia—De Divinatione* (New York: Putnam, 1922) pp. 108–211.

BLJ   Bernard of Clairvaux, *Letters*. Tr. B. S. James, *The Letters of St. Bernard of Clairvaux* (London: Burns Oates, 1953).

CC   Corpus christianorum, series Latina (Turnhout: Brepols, 1945–).

CCM   Corpus christianorum continuatio mediaevalis (Turnhout: Brepols, 1971–).

CF   Cistercian Fathers Series (Spencer, MA, Washington, DC: Cistercian Publications, 1970–).

Conf.   John Cassian, *Conferences*, SCh 42, 54, 64 (1955, 1958, 1959). Tr. G. Scannell, CS 20, 31.

Confessions   Augustine of Hippo, *Confessions*. Tr. J. G. Pilkington in *Basic Writings of Saint Augustine* (New York: Random House, 1948) 1:3–256.

CS   Cistercian Studies Series (Spencer, MA, Cistercian Publications, 1969–).

Duties   Ambrose of Milan, *Duties of the Clergy*. Tr. H. de Romestin in *Nicene and Post-Nicene Fathers*, series 2 (Grand Rapids, MI: Eerdmans, 1955) 10:1–89.

Ep   Letter(s).

Friends   A. M. Fiske, *Friends and Friendship in the Monastic Tradition*, Cidoc Cuaderno 51 (Cuernava-ca: CIDOC, 1970).

Iesu   Aelred of Rievaulx, *Jesus at the Age of Twelve*, CCM 1:249–278. Tr. Theodore Berkeley in *The Works of Aelred of Rievaulx*, CF 2:41–102.

Inst inclu   Aelred of Rievaulx, *A Rule of Life for a Recluse*, CCM 1:637–682. Tr. M. P. Macpherson in *The Works of Aelred of Rievaulx*, CF 2:41–102.

Life   Walter Daniel, *The Life of Aelred of Rievaulx*. Ed. and tr. F. M. Powicke (London: Nelson, 1950).

Monastic Order   David Knowles, *The Monastic Order in England*, 2nd ed. (Cambridge University, 1963).

OB   *Sancti Bernardi opera*. Ed. J. Leclercq, C. H. Talbot, H. M. Rochais (Rome: Editiones Cister-cienses, 1957–).

Oner   Aelred of Rievaulx, *Sermons on Isaiah*. PL 195: 363–500; CS 26.

PL   *Patrologiae cursus completus, series Latina* Ed. J.P. Migne (Paris, 1878–1890).

RB   *St. Benedict's Rule for Monasteries*, SCh 181, 182. Ed. Adalbert de Vogue (1972). Tr. Leonard Doyle (Collegeville: Liturgical Press, 1948).

SC   Bernard of Clairvaux, *Sermons on the Song of Songs*. OB 1 and 2. Tr. Kilian Walsh in *The Works of Bernard of Clairvaux*, CF4, 7, 31, 40.

SCh   Sources chrétiennes (Paris: Cerf, 1943–).

Spec car   Aelred of Rievaulx, *The Mirror of Charity*, CCM 1:3–161. Tr. Pierre Fortin in *The Works of Aelred of Rievaulx*, CF 17.

Spir amic   Aelred of Rievaulx, *Spiritual Friendship*, CCM 1:287–350. Tr. E. Laker in *The Works of Aelred of Rievaulx*, CF 5.

Notes

⬦

Introduction

1. The critical Latin edition of Aelred's *De spiritali amicitia* [*Spiritual Friendship*] appears in CCM 1:279–350. The English translation comes from Aelred of Rievaulx, *Spiritual Friendship*, Cistercian Fathers Series, no. 5, trans. Mary Eugenia Laker, with an Introduction by Douglass Roby (Kalamazoo, MI: Cistercian Publications, 1977). The treatise has been described as ". . . probably the most popular of all the early Cistercian texts." See Bernard McGinn, John Meyendorff, and Jean Leclercq, eds., *Christian Spirituality I: Origins to the Twelfth Century* (New York: Crossroad, 1985), 214.
2. For the Latin text and English translation, see Amic. See also Cicero, *De senectute, De amicitia, De divinatione*, The Loeb Classical Library (Cambridge, MA: Harvard University Press, 1923; reprint ed., 1979), 100–211.
3. Aelred of Rievaulx, *Spiritual Friendship* (1.1), 51 [CCM 1:289].
4. For the dialogue as a literary form, see Irwin Edman, ed., "Introduction" in *The Works of Plato* (New York: Tudor Publishing Company, 1931), xxiii–xxvi.
5. See above note 1.
6. For the English translation, see Walter Daniel, *The Life of Aelred of Rievaulx & Letter to Maurice*, CF 57, trans. F. M. Powicke with an Introduction by Marsha Dutton (Kalamazoo, MI: Cistercian Publications, 1994), 8–146. For the manuscript tradition and information on the medieval lives of Aelred, see 8–9. For a reflection of Aelred's in his works, see Charles Dumont, "Introduction," in Aelred of Rievaulx, *Mirror of Charity*, CF 15, trans. Elizabeth Connor (Kalamazoo, MI: Cistercian Publications, 1990), 20–44.
7. The information in this section comes from Douglass Roby, "Introduction," in Aelred of Rievaulx, *Spiritual Friendship*, 3–14; Dumont, "Introduction," in Aelred of Rievaulx, *Mirror of Charity*, 11–67; Aelred Squire, *Aelred of Rievaulx: A Study*, CS 50 (Kalamazoo, MI: Cistercian Publications, 1981), 1–71; John R. Sommerfeldt, *Aelred of Rievaulx: Pursuing Perfect Happiness* (New York: The Newman Press, 2005), 1–4; *The New Catholic Encyclopedia*, 2nd edition, vol. 1 (Detroit: Thomson-Gale, 2003), s.v. "Aelred (Ailred), St." by A. Hoste. The critical Latin edition of Aelred's spiritual works appears in CCM 1:1–763.
8. See C. H. Lawrence, *Medieval Monasticism: Forms of Religious Life in Western Europe in the Middle Ages*, 2nd ed. (London: Longman, 1989), 174–205; R. W. Southern, *Western Society and the Church in the Middle Ages* (New York: Penguin Books, 1970; 7th reprint ed., 1979), 254.
9. See *Exordium parvum*, nos. 15–17 in *Nomasticon Cisterciense seu antiquiores ordinis Cisterciensis constitutions*, eds. Juliano Paris and Hugone Séjalon (Solesme: E Typographeo Sancti Petri, 1892), 62–64; Squire, *Aelred of Rievaulx*, 28.
10. M.-D. Chenu, *Nature, Man, and Society in the Twelfth Century*, eds. Jerome Taylor and Lester K. Little (Chicago: The University of Chicago Press, 1968), 306.
11. See *The New Catholic Encyclopedia*, 2nd edition, vol. 1 (Detroit: Thomson-Gale, 2003), s.v. "Aelred (Ailred), St.," by A. Hoste; Bernard McGinn, John Meyendorff, and Jean Leclercq, eds., *Christian Spirituality I: Origins to the Twelfth Century* (New York: Crossroad, 1985), 214.
12. These five characteristics are treated in an expanded form in B.O. Gaybba, *Aspects of the Medieval History of Theology: 12th to 14th Centuries* (Pretoria: University of South Africa, 1988), 9–51. See also Dennis J. Billy, "Monastic Theology and Renewal of Catholic Moral Discourse: An Experiment in Historical Correlation," *Inter Fratres* 44(2004): 30–31.
13. See John R. Sommerfeldt, *Aelred of Rievaulx, On Love and Order in the World and Church* (New York: The Newman Press, 2006), 1–27. For Aelred's teaching on humanity's creation, fall, and redemption, see Sommerfeldt, *Aelred of Rievaulx: Pursuing Perfect Happiness*, 10–40. For his teaching on these themes in *On Spiritual Friendship*, see Dennis J. Billy, "The Healing Role of Friendship in Aelred of Rievaulx's *De spiritali amicitia*," *Studia moralia* 40(2002): 69–73.
14. See Sommerfeldt, *Aelred of Rievaulx, On Love and Order in the World and Church*, 28–36, 140–60.
15. See Charles Dumont, "Introduction," in Aelred of Rievaulx, *The Mirror of Charity*, 32–33.

16. See Roby, "Introduction," in Aelred of Rievaulx, *Spiritual Friendship*, 18. For Aelred's teaching on love and will, see Amédée Hallier, *The Theology of Aelred of Rievaulx: An Experiential Theology*, Cistercian Studies, no. 2 (Spencer, MA: Cistercian Publications, 1969), 26–33.
17. See Roby, "Introduction," in Aelred of Rievaulx, *Spiritual Friendship*, 18.
18. Ibid.
19. See Aelred of Rievaulx, *Spiritual Friendship* (1.1–69), 51–66 [CCM 1:289–301].
20. Ibid. (2.1–72), 69–87 [CCM 1:302–16].
21. Ibid. (3.1–134), 91–132 [CCM 1:317–50].
22. See *The Rule of Benedict*, Prologue, trans. Anthony C. Meisel and M.L. del Mastro (Garden City, NY: Image Books, 1975), 45. For an account of Aelred's conversion, see Dennis J. Billy, "Aelred of Rievaulx's Account of His Conversion in the *Liber de speculo caritatis*," *The American Benedictine Review* 52(2001): 239–54.
23. For a treatment of Aelred's sources, see Roby, "Introduction," to Aelred of Rievaulx, *Spiritual Friendship*, 29–35. See also the Index in Squire, *Aelred of Rievaulx*, 171[s.v. "Aelred (Ailred): patristic sources, classical sources"].
24. "The monks prefer to cultivate genres like the letter, the dialogue, and history in all its short forms from short chronicles and accounts of individual events to long annals." See Jean Leclercq, *The Love of Learning and the Desire for God*, trans. Catharine Misrahi (New York: Fordham University Press, 1982), 153–54.
25. For more on Aelred's use of the dialogue form, see Billy, "The Healing Role of Friendship," 64–69. See also above note 4.
26. For more on monastic reading, see Leclercq, *The Love of Learning and the Desire for God*, 15–17, 72–73; For monastic reading in Aelred, see Sommerfeldt, *Aelred of Rievaulx, On Love and Order in the World and Church*, 51–52.
27. For more on hierarchy, see Philip P. Wiener, ed., *Dictionary of the History of Ideas* (New York: Charles Scribner's Sons, 1973), s.v. "Hierarchy and Order," by C.A. Patrides. For the various hierarchies in Aelred's thought , see Sommerfeldt, , *Aelred of Rievaulx: On Love and Order in the World and Church*, 140–60.
28. For the interplay of the concepts of God, humanity, and the world, see N. Max Wildiers, *The Theologian and His Universe: Theology and Cosmology from the Middle Ages to the Present* (New York: The Seabury Press, 1982), 1–11. For Aelred's conceptions of God, humanity, and the world, see Sommerfeldt, *Aelred of Rievaulx: On Love and Order in the World and Church*, 1–7.
29. Aelred of Rievaulx, *Spiritual Friendship* (1.57), 63 [CCM 1:298–99].
30. For a summary of the different scholarly positions on Aelred's sexual orientation, see Sommerfeldt, *Aelred of Rievaulx: Pursuing Perfect Happiness*, 5–9. The literature includes: John Eastburn Boswell, *Christianity , Social Tolerance, and Homosexuality: Gay People in Western Europe from the Beginning of the Christian Era to the Fourteenth Century* (Chicago: University of Chicago Press, 1980); Brian Patrick McGuire, *Brother and Lover: Aelred of Rievaulx* (New York: Crossroad, 1994); Marsha L. Dutton, "The Invented Sexual History of Aelred of Rievaulx: A Review Article," *The American Benedictine Review* 47(1996): 414–32. For favorable and unfavorable reviews of McGuire's book, see Sommerfeldt, *Aelred of Rievaulx: Pursuing Perfect Happiness*, 142n.41.
31. Aelred of Rievaulx, *Spiritual Friendship* (1.10), 53 [CCM 1:291].

Prologue

1. Cf. Augustine, *Confessions* 2:2; 3:1: tr. J. G. Pilkington in *Basic Writings of St. Augustine* (New York: Random House, 1948) pp. 20, 29. It is not surprising to find right at the beginning of this dialogue on friendship the marked influence of St. Augustine, for none of the Fathers had so great an influence on the thinking of Aelred as did the Doctor of Hippo, especially through his *Confessions*. Walter Daniel in his *Life of Ailred* tells us that when Aelred was dying he ordered to be brought to him a Psalter, the *Confessions* of Augustine, and a text of St. John's Gospel, and told the assembled brethren: "Behold I have kept these by me in my little oratory and have delighted in them to the utmost as I sat alone there in times of leisure."—W. Daniel, *Life of Ailred*, tr. F. W. Powicke (New York: Nelson, 1950) p. 58. The very complete apparatus accompanying the critical edition of the *De spirituali amicitia* indicates on almost every line of this prologue some allusion to Augustine's *Confessions*. "To

love and to be loved," in the inverse order to what we find here but as it is in Augustine, is used by Aelred also in his *Mirror of Charity*, 1:25 (Cistercian Fathers Series, 17).

2. The reference is to Marcus Tullius Cicero, *De amicitia* sometimes called *Laelius*, which was written around the year 44 BC. Aelred borrows frequently from Cicero in this study on friendship, sometimes quoting him verbatim and indicating the borrowings. Other times he does not indicate them. While a list of parallel passages could be drawn up, there are yet pronounced differences. Aelred is far more systematic in his study of friendship, yet there is a rich, warm, personal touch in his presentation. The examples he chooses, too, are quite different from those of Cicero, who uses figures in Roman political life where Aelred draws on the scriptures. While for Cicero friendship was a social grace, for Aelred it is a means to Christian perfection. For a full study of Cicero's influence on Aelred, see J. Dubois' edition: *Aelred de Rievaulx: L'Amitié Spirituelle* (Paris: Beyaert, 1948) p. xlviii ff.

3. The experience that Aelred describes here is almost the exact opposite of that of Augustine in his earlier life as he describes it in the *Confessions: AC* 3:5, p. 33.

4. Cf. the reaction of St. Augustine to Cicero's *Hortensius*: "In the ordinary course of study, I lighted upon a certain book of Cicero, whose language, though not his heart, almost all admire. This book of his contains an exhortation to philosophy, and is called *Hortensius*. This book in truth, changed my affections . . . and since at that time (as you, O Lighted of my heart, know) the words of the Apostle were unknown to me, I was delighted with that exhortation, in so far only as I was thereby stimulated, and enkindled, and inflamed to love, seek, obtain, hold, and embrace, not this or that sect, but wisdom itself, whatever it were; and this alone checked me thus ardent that the name of Christ was not in it."— *Confessions* 3:4, p. 32. Perhaps Aelred's thought here is more directly influenced by Bernard of Clairvaux: Cf. *On the Song of Songs*, 15:6; CF 4:110: "But that name of Jesus is more than light, it is also food. . . . Every food of the mind is dry if it is not dipped in that oil; it is tasteless if not seasoned by that salt. Write what you will; I shall not relish it unless it tells of Jesus. Talk or argue about what you will, I shall not relish it if you exclude the name of Jesus. Jesus to me is honey in the mouth, music in the ear, a song in the heart."

5. Aelred gives here a clear outline of his work which he faithfully follows.

Book One

1. In the opening sentence of the dialogue, Aelred expresses succinctly the essence of Christian friendship, two men together with Christ as their bond.

2. Ivo is usually identified as a monk of Wardon in Bedforshire. He might have been sent there from Rievaulx sometime after 1135. Since Wardon was a foundation of Rievaulx, Aelred would have gone there at least once a year to make the regular visitation. It was at the request of Ivo (presumably the same person) that Aelred wrote his *Jesus at the Age of Twelve*. See *The Works of Aelred of Rievaulx*, vol. I (Cistercian Fathers Series 2); also *Ailred of Rievaulx, Christian Friendship* trans. H. Talbot (London: Catholic Book Club, 1942) p. 9: Dubois, *op. cit.* p. lxxiii.

3. See above Prologue, note 4, p. 46.

4. Amic 20.

5. In Latin a connection is seen between the words *caritas* (charity) and *carus* (precious).

6. Amic 26.

7. The *Speculum Caritatis, Mirror of Charity* (Cistercian Fathers Series 17), written by Aelred while he was still novice master of Rievaulx at the command of his Father Immediate (as Cistercians are accustomed to call the abbot of the motherhouse of their abbey), Bernard of Clairvaux. The third book especially of this work treats of friendship.

8. Isidore, *Etymologiae*, 10-5.

9. Rom 12:15.

10. Amic 81, 92. Cf. Spec car 3:39. Bernard of Clairvaux, Letter 53 (PL 182:160); tr. B. S. James, *The Letters of Bernard of Clairvaux* (London: Burns Oates, 1953), Letter 56, p. 84.

11. See Amic 32.

12. Prov 17:17. Aelred quotes this verse from Proverbs again in the third book, no. 63, where he teaches that the fidelity of a person should be tested before he is accepted into full

friendship. There he includes the second portion of the text: "He that is a friend loves at all times and a brother is proved in distress."

13. Amic 34.
14. See below, 3:39ff.
15. Prov 17:17.
16. Ibid.
17. St. Jerome, *Letters*, 3:6; PL 22:335.
18. Amic 15.
19. Cf. Julius Pomerius, *De vita contemplativa*, I. Prologue, 2 (PL 59:416), taken from the Pseudo-Seneca, *Monita*, 97.
20. Mt 7:7; Jn 16:24.
21. Cf. *Leonine Sacramentary*. 1229; ed. Mohlberg, p. 156, 17.
22. Ps 23:10.
23. Orestes, the son of Agamemnon, after the murder of his father was secretly taken to the home of his uncle Strophius. Here he was raised along with his cousin Pylades and a very deep bond of union and love grew up between these two cousins. Pylades helped Orestes to avenge the murder of his father and the two fled together. However, Orestes was condemned to death in the land of his exile. At this point Pylades proved the depth of his friendship by seeking to take the place of Orestes and die in his stead. Their friendship became proverbial, and they were even worshiped by the Scythians. It was Pacuvius who brought their legend into Latin literature. However Aelred probably knew it from Cicero (Amic 24) and Augustine (*Confessions* 4:6).
24. Acts 4:32.
25. Aelred is here repeating the definition of Cicero, adding however the significant adjective "complete."
26. St Ambrose, *On Virgins*, 2:4 (PL 16:224f.). Aelred repeats here what is evidently an error on the part of Ambrose. The reference seems undoubtedly to be to Theodora of Alexandria rather than of Antioch, whose story is related in the Martyrology (April 28th). Didyme is the "certain soldier." Actually he simply disguised himself as a soldier in order to save Theodora and for this paid the price of being beheaded.
27. Ps 39:6.
28. Jn 15:13.
29. Mt 5:44; Lk 6:27f.
30. Ps 10:6.
31. Cf. Spec car 3:2.
32. Cf. Cassian, *Conferences*, 16:2 (Cistercian Studies Series 31).
33. Cf. Ezek 16:25 and Jerome's commentary on this: *Commentary on Ezekiel*, 4:16 (PL 25:138).
34. Num 15:39.
35. *Idem velle et idem nolle*—this is a proverbial saying which Sallust places in the mouth of Cataline as he urges his fellow conspirators in the name of friendship to join him in revolt; *Cataline* 20:4; tr. J. Watson, *Sallust, Flores and Vellius Paterculus* (New York: Harper, 1885) p. 25.
36. Cf. Jerome, *Adv.Rufinum*. 1:1 7 (PL 23:430).
37. Sir 6:8.
38. No one seems to have been able yet to trace the source of this verse. Hoste (Spir amic, p. 176), Dubois (p. 29), Talbot (p. 135) all confess their ignorance as to the source.
39. Amic 31. Cf. Bernard of Clairvaux, *On the Song of Songs*, Sermon 83:4, OB 2:301; CF 40: "Love requires no other cause but itself, nor does it command a reward. Its reward is its enjoyment."
40. Jn 15:16f.
41. Amic 8,65. Cf. Conf. 16:3: "There is friendship which is constant and indissoluble, which is formed neither . . . in gifts received, nor in partnership in business, nor by instinct of nature, but which is cemented by likeness of manners or by the possession of the same virtues." SCh 54:224, CS 31. See also Chapter 5, ibid.
42. See above, note 35.
43. In his treatise on *Jesus at the Age of Twelve*, 20 (CF 2:27), Aelred brings out that the four cardinal virtues which he mentions here are nothing more than charity exercised in differ-

ent circumstances. Therefore true friendship is simply friendship which is animated by charity.

44. Amic 27.
45. Spec car 1:2.
46. Ps 15:2.
47. Amic 81.
48. Amic 81. Cf. Conf. 16:2.
49. Amic 69, 71. Cf. Bernard of Clairvaux, *On the Song of Songs*, Sermon 59:2 (CF 31). See below, note 57.
50. Gen 2:18.
51. Gen 2:21f.
52. St. Augustine, *On Free Will* 2:19.
53. St. Augustine, Sermon 47:9ff. (PL 38:303).
54. Cf. St. Bernard, SC 36:3; OB 2:5-6, CF 7.
55. Prov 17:17.
56. Jerome, Letter 3:6; PL 22:335.
57. Cf. 1 Jn 4:16.
58. Ibid.

Book Two

1. C. H. Talbot has an interesting note in regards to this "hair": "This seems to imply that Walter, though a monk, had no monastic tonsure. But during the first century of their existence, the Cistercians shaved tonsure and beard only seven times a year. This would allow Walter plenty of scope. In 1191 the number of shaving days was raised to nine, and in 1257 to twelve, reaching in 1293 twenty-five or six. This was a sign of relaxation frowned upon by the authorities, especially as the Dominicans, who lectured in the universities and who, presumably, would have to conform to the conventions of polite society, only shaved once every three weeks."—*op. cit.*, 138.
2. An allusion to Ex 5:14 which Aelred also uses in Spec car 1:18.
3. An ancient proverb which can be found, for example, in Xenophon, *Memorables*, , 1, 3, 5: see Marbodus. *Prouerb.* (PL 171:1736); H. Walther, *Prouerbia Sententiaque Latinitaitis Medii Aeui*, vol. 1 (Gottingen. 1936) p. 356.
4. Cf. Amic 102.
5. There is question here of an advisory reading prior to publication. See J. Leclercq, *Aspects litteraires de l'oeuvre de saint Bernard*, in *Cahiers de Civilis. Medíev.* 1 (1958) pp. 425-450. There we find the added injunction: "and do not give it to anyone to copy."—*Epistolae ad Seuerinum de caritate*, ed. G. Dumeige (Paris, 1955).
6. 1 Tim 4:8.
7. Amic 86. Cf. Bernard of Clairvaux, *Occasional Sermons I* 10:2; OB 6-1: 122–23—CF 46.
8. Eccles 4:10. Cf. Spec car, 2:39. See also St. Ambrose, *Duties* 3:131, p. 88.
9. Eccles 4:10.
10. Amic 22.
11. Sir 6:16.
12. St. Paul: Gal 6:2.
13. Amic 22.
14. Ibid.
15. Amic 23. Cf. Jerome, Ep 8:1; Bernard of Clairvaux, Ep 53; BLJ 56, p. 84; Ep 65:2; BLJ 68, p. 92ff.
16. Amic 23.
17. Jn 15:15.
18. See above, Prologue, note 1, p. 45.
19. We have no historical information concerning this Gratian. Indeed, he might well be a purely fictional character, although there is no objective reason to postulate this either. See Dubois, *op. cit.*, p. lxxxv.
20. Amic 26.
21. Cf. 2 Cor 13.

22. Acts 4:32.
23. Cor 6:17. Unity of spirit, being made one spirit with Christ, is a common theme among the Cistercian Fathers. See for example, William of St. Thierry, *On Contemplating God* 7, CF 3:47–48; *The Golden Epistle* 262–63; CF 12:95–96; Gilbert of Swineshead, *Sermons on the Song of Songs*, 32:8, PL 184-170; Aelred of Rievaulx, *A Rule of Life for a Recluse*, 26, CF 2:74. This unity of spirit whereby man is made to be one spirit with Christ is not of the ontological order or a unity of nature. It is rather a unity of wills or unity in charity. Bernard of Clairvaux makes this clear in his *Seventy-first Sermon on the Song of Songs*, no. 6: "The Word is in the Father and the Father is in the Word. Therefore, the union between them is in all respects perfect, and the Father and the Word are entirely and truly one. In this way, the soul for whom 'it is good to adhere to God' must not consider herself perfectly united to him until she has perceived that he abides in her and she in him. Not that she can say, even then, that she is one with God in the same sense in which the Father and the Word are one, although the Apostle assures us that 'he who is joined to the Lord is one spirit.' Thus we have scriptural authority for the unity of spirit between God and the soul, but not for any unity of nature . . . no creature whatever, whether of earth or heaven, unless one has taken leave of his senses, will dare to assert the words of the Only Begotten and presume to say, 'I and the Father are one.' On the other hand . . . I should not feel the slightest hesitation in saying that I was one spirit with God if only I were convinced that I adhered to him like one of those who abide in them. . . . It is to this kind of union that the Apostle refers, I think, when he says, 'He who is joined to the Lord is one spirit.' "—OB 2:218, CF 40.
24. Song 1:1.
25. Cf. Aelred's *Second Sermon for the Feast of the Epiphany* (CF 23); Bernard of Clairvaux, *On the Song of Songs*, 3, 4, 8, 9 (CF 4); Occasional Sermons, 10, 87 (CF 46). Walter Daniel, *Centum Sententiae*, 45, ed. C. H. Talbot, in *Sacris Erudiri* 11 (1960) p. 295f.
26. Cf. William of St. Thierry, *Exposition on the Song of Songs*, 30f, CF 6:25–26; *Meditations*, 8:5, CF 3:142.
27. Lk 23:12.
28. Spec car 1:34.
29. Cf. Pseudo-Ignatius, *Epist. ad Trallianos*, 13:3; ed. Funk, vol. 2, p. 113.
30. Cf. Quintillianus, *Institutio* 11:1.
31. Ps 132:1.
32. Song 1:1.
33. Ibid. 2:6.
34. See above, Part I, note 35, p. 59.
35. Amic 61.
36. These two last opinions are recounted by Cicero, but he does not indicate their authorship: Amic 56.
37. Jn 15:13.
38. Amic 18. Cf. John Cassian Conf, 16:3: "If then, you are desirous of lasting friendship, be diligent in cleansing your souls from all vice, and mortify your wills, that being united in the same desires and affections, you may attain to that peaceful state which David pronounces to be so pleasant and so happy: 'Behold how good and how pleasant it is for brethren to dwell together in unity.' "—SCh 54:226. "Hence the maxim of the Fathers: no friendship, no union, can be true except among persons solidly virtuous."—SCh 54:247, CS 31.
39. Amic 37, 40.
40. Gen 3:6.
41. 1 Sam 22:17f.
42. 2 Sam 13:3ff.
43. 2 Sam 15:12f.
44. Octavian Maledetti, an anti-pope who took the name of Victor IV, was elected in 1159 at the time of the death of Adrian IV. He had the support of Frederick I against Alexander III, the true Pope. The Cistercians remained faithful to Alexander III. See J. Canivez, *Statuta Capitulorum Generalium Ordinis Cisterciensis ab anno 1116 ad annum 1786*, vol. 1 (Louvain, 1933), p. 73. John of St. Martin, a Cardinal Priest, had concurred in the election of Octavian. Octavian died on April 20, 1164. Cardinal Guido de Crene succeeded him and took the name of Pascal III. Otto was a Cardinal who belonged to the group supporting Guido.

This passage is important for helping us date the writing of the *Spiritual Friendship*. *See the Introduction in Dubois, op. cit.* p. xcii.

45. Amic 18.
46. Ibid. This is a reference to some of the ideas of the Stoics.
47. Cf. Amic 50; Bernard of Clairvaux, Ep 270-3; BLJ 340, p. 419.
48. Titus 2:12.
49. Amic 40.
50. Amic 39.
51. Walter here presents rather succinctly the position of the Stoics. See Seneca's *Letter to Lucilius*, 9:1; trans. R. M. Gummere, *The Epistles of Seneca.* vol. I, Loeb Classical Series (New York: Putnam, 1925). p. 43.
52. Amic 45.
53. Amic 59.
54. Amic 45. Here Aelred reproduces Cicero almost word for word and Cicero in his turn is but translating Euripides, *Hippolytus,* 253ff, tr. A. Way, Loeb Classical Series, vol. 4 (New York: Putnam, 1922), p. 181.
55. Amic 47. Where Aelred speaks of "God," Cicero speaks of "the immortal gods."
56. Amic 48. Cf. Augustine, *The City of God,* 19:8.
57. 2 Cor 11:28f.
58. Rom 9:2f.
59. 1 Thes 2:7.
60. Col 1:28.
61. 2 Tim 2:25.
62. 2 Cor 11:3.
63. 2 Cor 2:4.
64. 2 Cor 12:21.
65. 2 Sam 16:15ff.; 17:5ff.
66. Amic 79. Cf. Conf 16:28: "It has also been shown by experience that friendships begun . . . without a desire for perfection, or for fulfilling the apostolic precept of charity, but for satisfying earthly love . . . cannot long preserve their unity unbroken." —SCh 54:246–47, CS 31.
67. Spec car 1:25.
68. Cf. Augustine, *Confessions* 2:2; 3:1.
69. The experience of sweetness which is granted to those who begin to follow the ways of virtue, and in this case spiritual friendship, is a characteristic note in the spirituality described by the Cistercians.
70. While Cicero in his *De inventione*, 2:55, allowed for a type of friendship based on such motivations as are expressed here, he later in Amic (25, 50) rejected this as not being true friendship and developed the line of thinking which Aelred presents here. However, in this instance Aelred is undoubtedly also influenced by Augustine, Sermon 385:4 (PL 39:1692): "The love of friendship should be gratuitous. You ought not to have or to love a friend for what he will give you. If you love him for the reason that he will supply you with money or some other temporal favor, you love the gift rather than him. Friends should be loved freely for themselves and not for anything else."
71. Amic 30. Cf. Bernard of Clairvaux, *On the Song of Songs*, 83:5, OB 2:301, CF 40; *On Loving God.* 7:17, OB 3:134, CF 13: "True love is its own fulfillment. It has a reward, but it is the possession of the object it loves . . . true love asks no reward, but deserves one."
72. Amic 30.
73. 2 Sam 17:27f. Compare this to what Cicero has to say (Amic 30) concerning Scipio and Lelius. See also Spec car 3:13.
74. 2 Sam 19:31ff.
75. Amic 30.
76. I Sam 19–20; 2 Sam 9.
77. Amic 51.
78. Acts 4:32

Book Three

1. This passage finds a parallel in Spec car 3:20: "There is love proceeding from affection when the mind surrenders itself to feeling; love proceeding from reason, when the will unites itself to reason, and there may be a third kind of love compounded from these two when, for instance, reason, feeling, and will unite together. The first kind of love is delightful but dangerous, the second is dry but fruitful; the third kind possesses the advantages of them both, and alone is perfect. To the first love one is enticed by the experience of sweetness; to the second kind of love one is driven by cold reason; but in the third love, reason itself finds pleasure."

2. See below, note 54. Cf. also Amic 20; Spec car 1:33; 3:4, 19; Bernard of Clairvaux, *On Loving God*, 26, OB 3:140, CF 13: Ep 271, BLJ, Ep 341, pp. 419f.

3. *Duties* 133: "For what is a friend but a partner in love, to whom you unite and attach your soul and with whom you blend so as to desire from being two to become one, to whom you entrust yourself as to a second self, from whom you fear nothing, and from whom you demand nothing dishonorable for the sake of your own advantage."

4. Amic 67; *Duties* 127. Cf. also Cicero, *Timaeus*, 6.

5. *Duties* 127.

6. Cf. Conf. 16:24: "Charity cannot be made stable and undisturbed except among men of the same degree of virtue and of the same purpose."—SCh 54:243, CS 31.

7. Amic 20.

8. Amic 65.

9. See above, Book One, note 35, p. 59.

10. Sir 6:9.

11. Prov 22:24f.

12. Eccles 7:10.

13. Sir 22:27. See below, note 56, p. 108.

14. Sir 22:26f.

15. Sir 22:27. It would be well to note here that Aelred is following the Vulgate which has two distinct words which are translated here as: "upbraiding and reproach"; whereas the Greek text, which the Revised Standard Version (22:22) follows, has only one term.

16. Sir 27:17.

17. Sir 27:24.

18. Eccles 10:11.

19. 2 Sam 16:3ff; 1 Kings 2:8f.

20. 1 Sam 25:10, 38.

21. 1 Chron 19:1ff.; 2 Sam 10:1ff; 12:26ff.

22. 2 Sam 15:12ff.; 17:1ff.

23. Num 12:1ff.

24. Amic 62.

25. RB 64:16.

26. Ps 139:2; Job 11:2.

27. Prov 29:20 (Septuagint).

28. *Duties* 132. Cf. Amic 50.

29. Cf. Conf. 16:18: "There is another abuse committed by some who think they are patient. . . . We do not reply to our brethren when they provoke us. This grave and affected silence . . . irritates them infinitely more than the most sarcastic speech or injurious words." —SCh 54:237–39, CS 31. Also, Seneca, *De ira*, 13:8; tr. A. Stewart, "Of Anger," *Minor Dialogues* (London: Ball, 1889) p. 83.

30. Amic 79.

31. Amic 76.

32. Cato as quoted in Amic 76. Cf. Cicero, *De officiis*, 1:120; Seneca, *Epist. ad Lucil.*, 22; Jerome, Ep 8 (PL 22:342).

33. Amic 76.

34. Amic 78.

35. Amic 77.

36. Lesu 21; CF 2:28–29; Ohner 8, PL 195:3890, CF 26.

37. Amic 78.

38. Prov 17:17.
39. Esther 7.
40. Jgs 4:17ff.
41. 2 Sam 21:1ff.
42. Jerome, Ep 3:6, PL 22:335.
43. Spec car 3:40.
44. Sir 22:27. See above, note 15.
45. *Duties* 129, p. 88; Cf. Bernard of Clairvaux, Ep 125:1. BLJ 128, p. 190.
46. Prov 14:20.
47. Prov 17:17.
48. Prov 25:19.
49. Lk 16:10. Aelred actually does not give the text verbatim but changes *in minimo* to *in modico* and *majori* to *in multo*.
50. Dubois identifies this friend with the one Aelred speaks of below, note 124— *L'amitié* p. 139, no. 1.
51. Dubois identifies this sacristan of Clairvaux as Blessed Gerard, the brother of St. Bernard— ibid.
52. Amic 79.
53. Amic 80.
54. Mt 22:39.
55. Ibid. Cf. Seneca, *De Moribus,* 20; Bernard of Clairvaux, Ep 53, BIJ 56, p. 84.
56. *Duties* 3:133, p. 89.
57. *Duties* 134, ibid.
58. Amic 82.
59. Amic 88.
60. Sir 6:16.
61. Amic 62. The same idea is found in Xenophon, *Memorables,* 2:4.
62. Amic 63.
63. Cf. Cicero, *Pro Plancio,* 80; tr. N. H. Watts, *Cicero, The Speeches,* Loeb Classical Series (Cambridge: Harvard, 1935) p. 513.
64. Amic 87: "This especially would be granted if it could happen that God should remove us from the companionship of men and place us somewhere in solitude, and there provide us with an abundance of those things that nature craves for, taking away, at the same time, all hope of seeing a fellow creature. Who would have such a heart of steel as not to find such existence intolerable? Who would not lose enjoyment in all other pleasures in such solitude?"
65. Ps 8:8f.
66. Amic 62.
67. Amic 52.
68. Cf. Spec car 1:34; *De Bello Standardii* (PL 195:708).
69. Spec car 1:34. See above, note 29.
70. Ps 132:1.
71. Jn 15:15.
72. Ibid.
73. Jn 15:14.
74. *Duties* 135, p. 89.
75. *Duties* 4:8f, p. 48f.
76. Amic 22.
77. The theme of "illumination" is a common one among the Cistercians who undoubtedly draw upon St. Augustine for this. For a study of this theme, see J. Morson and H. Costello, Introduction, in *The Liturgical Sermons of Guerric of Igny,* vol. 1, CF 8:xxxviii–xlvi.
78. Amic 65.
79. Cf. ibid.
80. Cf. Spec car 1:34; *Third Sermon for the Feast of the Epiphany* (CF 23); *Second Sermon for the Feast of the Annunciation* (ibid.); Cassidorus, *De anima,* 13, ed. J. W. Halporn in *Traditio* 16 (1960) p. 39.
81. Amic 66.

82. Amic 69. Jerome, *Commentary on Matthew*, 2:7 (PL 25:1219). Cf. Augustine, *De Genesi ad litteram imperfectus liber*, 18 (PL 34:243); also Jerome on Micah, c. 8: "Friendship either finds equals or makes them. Where there is inequality, one takes pre-eminence, and the other bears subjection. But this is not so much friendship as adulation. Hence we read somewhere: 'Let your friend be as your own soul.' And the poet, praying for his friend, says, 'preserve the half of my soul.'"(PL 25:1218f.).
83. 2 Cor 8:15. Cf. Ex 16:18.
84. Amic 72. Cf. *Duties* 3:132, p. 88f.
85. I Sam 20; Cf. Spec car 3:12, 29.
86. 1 Sam 23:17.
87. Ibid.
88. I Sam 20:32; 19:5.
89. 1 Sam 20:30.
90. 1 Sam 20:31.
91. 1 Sam 23:17.
92. Amic 63.
93. Amic 64.
94. 1 Sam 23:17.
95. Lk 10:37.
96. Sir 6:16.
97. *Duties* 3:128, p. 88.
98. Amic 44.
99. Sir 29:13.
100. Eph 1:22f, 5:30; Gal 1:18.
101. Ps 24:15.
102. Jas 1:5.
103. Amic 44.
104. Acts 4:32.
105. Ruth 2:8ff.
106. Pseudo-Seneca, *Monita,* 97.
107. Amic 82.
108. Amic 44.
109. Terence, *Andria,* 68; ed. J. Marouzeau, vol. 1 (Paris, 1947) p. 128; tr. P. Perry, *The Comedies of Terence* (London: Milford, 1929) p. 6.
110. Amic 89.
111. Amic 88–90.
112. Prov 27:6. Amic 91.
113. *Duties* 3:127, p. 88.
114. Amic 91.
115. Amic 92. Cf. Bernard of Clairvaux, Ep 78:13, BLJ 80, p. 118; Ep 35, BLJ 36, p. 70.
116. Ps 145:5.
117. Is 3:12.
118. Prov 11:9.
119. Wis 11:24.
120. Ezek 33:11.
121. Terence, *Eunuchus,* 252; ed. J. Marouzeau, vol. 1 (Paris, 1947) p. 239; tr. P. Perry, *The Comedies of Terence* (London: Milford, 1929) p. 140. Aelred probably received this directly from Cicero (Amic 93); however it is possible that he himself read Terence as he was widely read in the monasteries during the Middle Ages. He was frequently cited by Augustine and this would be another possible source for Aelred. Gnatho was a type of the parasitical sycophant.
122. Is 30:10.
123. Jer 5:31.
124. See Inst incl. 1, CF 2:44.
125. 2 Sam 12:1ff.
126. Cf. Spec car 3:38.
127. Amic 73.

128. Cf. Conf. 16:14: "Friendship is for a few, and only for those who by identity of tastes and similarity of virtues are united to us. This is evidently referred to in what the Gospel says of St. John the Evangelist, 'the disciple whom Jesus loved'; since he certainly loved with a special affection the other eleven who had been chosen by him . . ." Cf. Spec car 3:39.—SCh 54:233–34, CS 31.
129. Jn 19:26f.
130. Mt 16:19.
131. Cf. Inst incl. 31, CF 2:87.
132. Jn 13:21ff.
133. Jn 21:22.
134. Jn 13:15.
135. Amic 79.
136. Cf. Spec car 3:18: "For this is rightly ordered affection: not to love what is not to be loved; to love what is to be loved; but not to love in a greater measure than what is due; not to love with equal affection those things which should be loved in different degrees; not to love in different measure those things that should be equally loved." Cf. Bernard of Clairvaux, Ep 85:3, BLJ 87, p. 162: ". . . that I may see and rejoice at the rightly ordered charity in me, knowing and loving what ought to be loved, as much as they should be loved, and for the reason that they should be loved; being unwilling also to be loved except in you, and only in so far as I should be loved."
137. Amic 102.
138. Cf. *Confessions* 4:4. This first friend is usually identified as Aelred's beloved Simon whose death wrung from him the very heartfelt lament which we find in Spec car 1:34.
139. Powicke identifies this second friend as being Geoffrey of Dinant whom Aelred brought back to Rievaulx when he returned from Rome in 1142; see F. M. Powicke, *Aelred of Rievaulx and his Biographer Walter Daniel* (Manchester: Longmans Green and Co., 1922) p. 50; see also Dubois, *L'amitié*, p. lxxxviii.
140. Cf. Sallust, *Catilina,* 5:3; Watson, p. 10.
141. Ps 37:14.
142. Ps 72:22.
143. Abbot Maurice who had resigned as Abbot of Rievaulx in 1147.
144. Cf. *Confessions* 7:21.
145. Cf. Spec car 129.
146. Cf. Bernard of Clairvaux, Ep 85, BLJ 87. pp. 125ff.
147. Amic 45.
148. Acts 4:32.
149. See above, 1:40, note 35.
150. A common image coming from antiquity. It is found already in Xenophon, *Memorables,* 2:4.
151. Tob 5:23.
152. See above, Prologue, note 1, p. 45.
153. Cf. Augustine, *Soliloquies,* 1:8; tr. C. Starbuck in *Basic Writings of Saint Augustine,* vol. 1 (New York: Random House, 1948) p. 263.
154. Ps 132:1.
155. Gal 6:2.
156. See above, note 101. Cf. Augustine, Ep 145:7; 186:41; 20:2.
157. Ps 33:9; 99:5. Cf. Oner 3, PL 195:371A, CF 26; Lesu 1:8, CF 2:12; Walter Daniel, *Centum Sententiae, 79, loc. cit.* pp. 344ff.
158. 1 Cor 15:54f.
159. 1 Cor 15:28.

Suggested Readings

⁂

By Aelred of Rievaulx

Aelred of Rievaulx. *Dialogue on the Soul*. Translation and Introduction by C. H. Talbot. CF 22. Kalamazoo, MI: Cistercian Publications, 1981.
_____. *Mirror of Charity*. Translated by Elizabeth Connor. Introduction and Notes by Charles Dumont. CF 17. Kalamazoo, MI: Cistercian Publications, 1990.
_____. *Spiritual Friendship*. Translated by Mary Eugenia Laker. Introduction by Douglass Roby. CF 5. Kalamazoo, MI: Cistercian Publications, 1977.
_____. *Spiritual Friendship*. Translated by Mark Williams. Scranton, PA: University of Scranton Press, 2005.
_____. *Treatises and Pastoral Prayer*. Introduction by David Knowles. CF 2. Kalamazoo, MI: Cistercian Publications, 1971.

Studies

Brooke, Odo. "Monastic Theology in St. Aelred." In *Studies in Monastic Theology*, pp. 219–25. CS 37. Kalamazoo, MI: Cistercian Publications, 1980.
_____. "Towards a Theology of Connatural Knowledge," *Citeaux* 18(1967): 275–90.
Burridge, A. "The Spirituality of St. Aelred." *Downside Review* 58(1940): 225–47.
Dumont, Charles. "Aelred of Rievaulx's *Spiritual Friendship*." In *Cistercian Ideals and Reality*, pp. 187–98. Edited by John R. Sommerfeldt. CS 60. Kalamazoo, MI: Cistercian Publications, 1978.
_____. "St. Aelred: The Balanced Life of a Monk," *Monastic Studies* 1(1963): 25–38.
Dutton, Marsha L. "Aelred of Rievaulx on Friendship, Chastity and Sex: the Sources." *Cistercian Studies Quarterly* 29(1994): 121–96.
Hallier, Amédée. *The Monastic Theology of Aelred of Rievaulx: An Experiential Theology*. Translated by Columban Heaney. CS 2. Shannon, Ireland: Irish University Press, 1969.
Heaney, Columban. "Aelred of Rievaulx: His Relevance to the Post-Vatican II Age." In *The Cistercian Spirit: A Symposium in Honor of Thomas Merton*, pp. 166–89. CS 3. Edited by M. Basil Pennington. Spencer, MA: Cistercian Publications, 1970.
Jarrett, Bede. "St. Aelred of Rievaulx." In *The English Way*, pp. 81–103. Edited by Maisie Ward. New York: Sheed and Ward, 1934.
La Corte, Daniel M. "Aelred of Rievaulx's Doctrine of Grace and Its Role in the *Reformatio* of the Soul." In *Praise No Less than Charity: Studies in Honor of M. Chrysogonus Waddell, Monk of Gethsemani Abbey*. Edited by E. Rozanne Elder. CS 193. Kalamazoo, MI: Cistercian Studies, 2002.
Merton, Thomas. "St. Aelred and the Cistercians." Edited by Patrick Hart. *Cistercian Studies* 20(1985): 212–25; 21(1986): 30–42; 22(1987): 55–75; 23(1988): 45–62; 24(1989): 50–68.
Sommerfeldt, John R. *Aelred of Rievaulx: On Love and Order in the World and Church*. New York/Mahwah, NJ: The Newman Press, 2006.
_____. *Aelred of Rievaulx: Pursuing Perfect Happiness*. New York/Mahwah, NJ: The Newman Press, 2005.
_____. "The Roots of Aelred's Spirituality: Cosmology and Anthropology." *Cistercian Studies Quarterly* 38(2003): 19–26.
Squire, Aelred. *Aelred of Rievaulx: A Study*. CS 50. Kalamazoo, MI: Cistercian Publications, 1981.
_____. Aelred of Rievaulx and the Monastic Tradition concerning Action and Contemplation." *Downside Review* 72(1954): 289–303.

Analytic Index

✛

The first number refers to the book; the number(s) after the colon refer to the sections within the book.

About the Dedication

✛

J. Alan Groves (1952–2007) was Professor of Old Testament at Westminster Theological Seminary in Philadelphia and founder of the Westminster Hebrew Institute (recently renamed the J. Alan Groves Center for Advanced Biblical Research). He was internationally known for his work in the application of computer technology to the study and teaching of the Hebrew Bible and language. In addition to being an eminent scholar, teacher, pastor, and administrator, he also had a profound love for God, family, and friends. His wife Libbie and his children—Alasdair, Rebeckah, Eowyn, and Alden—can easily attest to that, as can the many friends he made while a student at Dartmouth College (1971–1976), a pastor of the Congregational Church in West Fairlee, Vermont (1976–1979), and a student and later Professor and Academic Dean at Westminster (1979–2007). Al was a friend of Christ and extended that friendship to others. Everything he did flowed from his love of God and desire to share that love with others.

Dennis J. Billy, C.Ss.R. is a teacher, writer, and poet. Ordained a Redemptorist priest in 1980, he taught the history of moral theology and Christian spirituality at the Alphonsian Academy of Rome's Pontifical Lateran University for more than twenty years, reaching the rank of Ordinary Professor. He currently holds The John Cardinal Krol Chair of Moral Theology as a scholar-in-residence at St. Charles Borromeo Seminary in Philadelphia. He also serves as The Karl Rahner Professor of Catholic Theology at the Graduate Theological Foundation in South Bend, Indiana. Father Billy is the author of numerous books and articles, both popular and scholarly. Raised in Staten Island, New York, and educated there through high school in local Catholic schools, he graduated from Dartmouth College and went on to receive four master's degrees, as well as doctorates from Harvard University, the Pontifical University of St. Thomas, and the Graduate Theological Foundation.

⁌

Aelred of Rievaulx was born in 1110 near modern-day Scotland. He came from a long line of married priests, but saw his family's traditional profession end when Rome declared mandatory celibacy for all priests. Well-connected among the nobility, he first became an influential member of the court of King David I of Scotland. It was here that he read Cicero's *On Friendship*. Although Aelred was both successful and popular at court, he was unhappy with his life of luxury, and discontent with the superficial nature of his ties. He yearned for something more. In 1134, while on his return from a mission to the archbishop of York, Aelred visited the newly established Cistercian monastery of Rievaulx. Aelred was so impressed with what he saw that within two days he found himself again at the monastery gate seeking admission and was accepted. Aelred flourished in his new monastic setting just as he did at the court of King David. In 1147, he was elected abbot of Rievaulx, a position he would hold until his death in 1167.

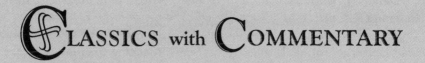

Visits to the Most Holy Sacrament and to Most Holy Mary

Alphonsus de Liguori
The Classic Text Translated and with a Spiritual Commentary
Dennis Billy, C.Ss.R.

The first complete and faithful English translation from its original Italian of *Visits to the Most Holy Sacrament and to Most Holy Mary*, a devotional classic by St. Alphonsus de Liguori. *Father Dennis Billy has retrieved for us a spiritual classic with his insightful introduction, instructive commentary, and a clear and strong translation.* —**Lawrence S. Cunningham**, John A. O'Brien Professor of Theology, The University of Notre Dame

ISBN: 9780870612442 / 160 pages / $15.95

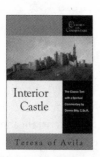

Interior Castle

Teresa of Avila
The Classic Text with a Spiritual Commentary
Dennis Billy, C.Ss.R.

The classic E. Allison Peers translation of this Christian favorite is united with fresh spiritual commentary, making it the only edition of Teresa of Avila's classic to remain faithful to her mystical vision while providing spiritual nourishment.

ISBN: 9780870612411 / 320 pages / $16.95

The Imitation of Christ

Thomas À Kempis
A Spiritual Commentary and Reader's Guide
Dennis Billy, C.Ss.R.

Fr. Billy highlights how today's Christians can interpret and apply *The Imitation* to their own spiritual journeys with the help of William Creasy's accessible translation. Billy opens each chapter with a brief introduction and completes each one with reflection questions to help readers apply the text to their lives.

ISBN: 9780870612343 / 272 pages / $15.95

Christian Classics™
from Ave Maria Press, Inc.   Notre Dame, IN
www.avemariapress.com

Keycode: FD9Ø6Ø8ØØØØ